Model Sailing Ships

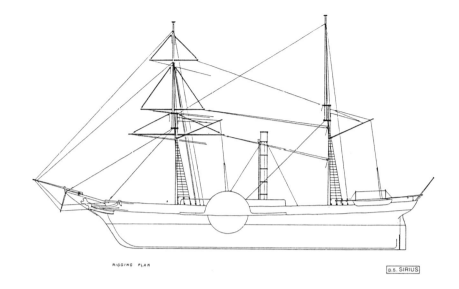

RIGGING PLAN

D.S. SIRIUS

Model Sailing Ships

DESIGN AND CONSTRUCTION

Robert F. Brien

B.T. Batsford Ltd   London

Acknowledgements

The author and publishers would like to thank the Science Museum, Kensington, London for their kind permission to photograph and publish Figures 2, 3, 4, 5, 6, 28 and 39. Particular thanks are due to the Curator of the Water Transport Section of the Science Museum, Mr Joe Roome, for his interest, advice and encouragement. Much of the author's initial interest in the subject was engendered by the enthusiasm of the late Ron Blackman, a modelmaker of extraordinary talent. The author's special thanks are due to his wife, Amber, who showed great patience and forbearance in typing the manuscript.

© Robert F. Brien 1986
First published 1986

ISBN 0 7134 4894 6

Typeset by Servis Filmsetting Ltd, Manchester
and printed in Great Britain by Anchor-Brendon Ltd
Tiptree, Essex
for the publishers
B.T. Batsford Ltd
4 Fitzhardinge Street
London W1H 0AH

Contents

Introduction

An attempt to cover every aspect of the construction of all types of ship models in one slim volume would be so superficial that the reader would be left both confused and frustrated, and the enthusiasm which led him to obtain the book in the first instance would be diminished. This book, therefore, is confined to giving very detailed information on procedures likely to be encountered in the basic construction of most models of sailing ships of the square rigger variety, with emphasis on the eighteenth and nineteenth centuries rather than earlier periods. Sources of information on this type of vessel are given, and methods, materials and tools are described, as well as hints on the display of the completed model. Finally, a set of building plans for the paddle steamer *Sirius* is included as an appendix (*pp. 111–16*).

Some modellers are, understandably, a little reluctant to part readily with hard-earned methods developed over years of trial and error. Yet it is interesting to find how often several modellers working independently arrive at the same conclusion as to the best means of achieving a particular result. Method, then, is only part of the requirement, the other component being skill; and you, the reader, will know whether you possess enough of this talent to develop it in the field of model sailing ships.

What is the attraction of ship modelling in comparison with models of other types? It has been a much-respected craft for some centuries, particularly by the British and Dutch; and one is immediately led to connect these countries with their need to defend themselves from attack from the sea, and their consequent development as seafaring nations. Interest in the sea thus became a national characteristic, undoubtedly resulting in much of the world's progress in maritime development.

Then there is the challenge of seeing a fine model. In taking up the challenge one quickly learns that by far the greatest cost lies in *time*, for the materials in the quantities needed represent a very modest outlay, and tools tend to build up over a long period, so that their cost is unnoticed. The main ingredient of the model will be you, the modeller, your skills in a surprising number of diverse fields, and your ability to adapt your talents to the fascinating demands of a wide variety of constructional problems. Nothing is easy, however simple the result may appear, but the satisfaction which comes from seeing the moderately successful outcome of one's efforts acts as a spur in the determination to improve with practice. It is rare for a modeller to be wholly satisfied with his completed work, particularly after the passage of time; but each model becomes a little better and moves further towards the goal of perfection.

1. Selecting a model to build

It is probable that one would always choose to build a model of an actual ship in preference to one representing only a type or class. If this is accepted, then clearly the model must reflect as closely as possible not only the general appearance of the vessel, but also the detailed construction down to the smallest deck fitting, with great attention being paid to scale. Here lies the great difficulty, in that accurate records of ships become increasingly difficult to track down as the date of their origin becomes more remote. The earlier the vessel, the more likely is the information available to be questionable. More recent ships may have detailed plans, pictures and even photographs lodged with maritime museums or other interested bodies, where models may be on display. These are an excellent starting-point for the modelmaker, but it will still be necessary to carry out cross-checking before you can be reasonably sure of your facts. Reference is made later to the construction of a model of the *Great Western* of which there is a fine ¼in scale model in the Science Museum, Kensington; but in Donald McNarry's book, *Ship Models in Miniature*, he draws attention to photographs of contemporary pictures which show a forecastle deck level with the bulwarks, something which does not appear on the model.

Perhaps only where a number of cross-references agree, or where the original vessel itself has been preserved, can you really be certain that you are building an accurate representation. Models which fall outside this category may be called 'conjectural', and it must be accepted that even if much that is shown is close to the reality of the original, there are areas where informed or inspired guesswork has been employed. The extent of this is up to the modelmaker, who must set his own limits and abide by his own standards.

There is no need to be discouraged by the foregoing, and the beginner should simply bear this factor in mind while directing his enthusiasm towards considering a suitable subject for his modelmaking efforts. It is recommended that the inexperienced model shipwright should avoid a very complex model, as the length of time it will take to complete may prove too severe a test of his patience. The exercise, if it is to be done at all properly, is going to take a long time: many months, perhaps even years. There is no doubt that a beautifully-built simple model will give infinitely more satisfaction and draw far more acclaim than a rapidly-constructed model on which much of the detail is of poor quality.

TYPES OF MODEL

There are four basic ways of representing a ship in model form, the term for each being more or less self-explanatory:

Full hull models (*Figure 1*)

These show the vessel complete in every detail, with all deck fittings and fixtures, all spars and rigging, and with or without sails; and would show how the ship would have looked at the time of her completion. The model would normally be displayed in a glass case, resting on some form of decorative cradle or attractive props.

Admiralty Board dockyard models (*Figure 2*)

These usually have the planking omitted below the waterline to show the ribs and keel construction, and areas of deck are left unplanked in order to give a clear indication of what happens below this level. The original object of this type of model was to show the commissioners exactly what they were getting for their money, and so it must be borne in mind that virtually everything will have to be shown if this category of model is chosen.

Figure 1 A full hull model of the paddle steamer *Sirius* (1837). This was the first vessel to cross the Atlantic from London to New York under continuous steam power.

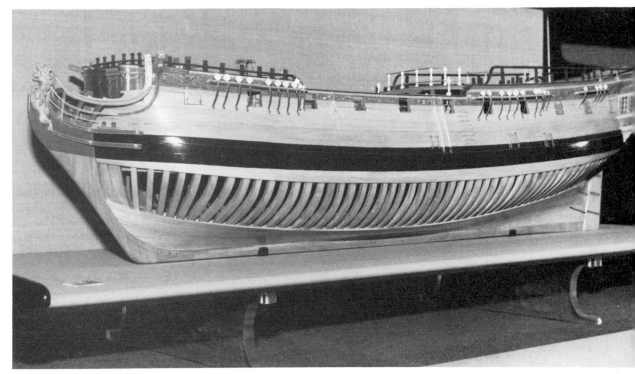

Figure 2 Admiralty Board dockyard model of a 20-gun sixth-rate ship (1745). The planking below the waterline has been omitted to reveal the frames.

Figure 3 A waterline model set in a realistically-sculpted sea.

Waterline models (*Figure 3*)

This type shows the full details of the vessel from the waterline upwards, and rests in a simulated sea. The whole display gives a realistic impression of the ship, possibly standing with bare masts at a calm mooring, or heeling in a tempestuous sea with gale-filled sails.

Scenic models (*Figure 4*)

These go beyond waterline models in that they depict some real or imagined event in the life of the ship. The modelling extends further than just the vessel and its immediate environment, and may show a busy dockside with figures loading a cargo, or perhaps Captain Bligh being set adrift by his mutinous crew.

Figure 4 A scenic model depicting a busy dock-yard scene.

DRAWINGS AND PAINTINGS BY MARINE ARTISTS

There is a wealth of information available on ships from the works of artists going back over many centuries, and clearly here is a source from which data may be checked even if it does not form the basis of model construction. However, it must be stressed again that cross-checking is essential, and that on no account should a single illustration be considered the whole truth. An example is J. Th. De Bry's volume *The Great Voyages* published about 1590, which contains unusually fine engravings of a wide range of ships; yet even the inexperienced eye can detect anachronisms in the costume of characters depicted. Closer inspection reveals that some ships are a whole century more modern than those they are purported to represent, and at this point the researcher reluctantly turns away to some

more reliable source of information, because painters of this period had little if any seafaring experience on which to base their portrayal of ships.

It is not until the seventeenth century that some degree of accuracy can be gleaned from the study and comparison of drawings and paintings executed by competent artist historians. Some of the most famous of these are listed below.

Van de Velde the Elder (1611–1693) and **Van de Velde the Younger** (1633–1707). This Dutch father-and-son combination produced work of superb artistic merit as well as accurately recording practical details of a great number of ships over the considerable period in which they served in the Dutch fleet.

Jean Bérain (1640–1711). An artist at the court of Louis XIV in the latter part of the seventeenth century, he was involved in the decorative design of a number of ships commissioned by Colbert, the Navy Minister, and his work is preserved in the *Service Hydrographique de la Marine* in Paris. His drawings are particularly valuable in that they show, in addition to meticulously-detailed vessels, contemporary methods of construction, launching and fitting out.

Frederic-Henry Chapman (1721–1808), the Swedish master shipwright, was responsible for the classification of contemporary European merchantmen, and published *Architectura Navalis Mercatoria* in 1768, acknowledged among the finest collections of eighteenth-century maritime drawings. They were the result of dedicated study and enquiry, and show an immense amount of detail, including sheerline and elevational drawings of exceptional quality.

Pierre Ozanne (early eighteenth century), who served in the French navy for 59 years, left a legacy of fine drawings showing, among other details, how vessels were rigged under various weather conditions.

James Cleveley (1750–1823) accompanied Captain Cook on his first voyage, and illustrated much of what was experienced in line-and-wash drawings or watercolour. Many paintings were made of *Resolution* and *Discovery*, and comparison of these indicate that they are accurate records of the details of these vessels.

Antoine Roux (1765–1835) and **F. Roux** of Marseilles produced between them a large number of maritime paintings abounding in accurate detail and devoid of artistic whim, and depicting the principles of sailing and the life of the sailor in the early to mid-nineteenth century in a manner which suggests genuineness and great understanding. Frequently two views of a vessel are included in the same painting so that as much as possible of the design is visible.

HISTORICAL DEVELOPMENT OF SAILING SHIPS

The main factors which determined the shape of the hulls and the configuration of the rigging as shipbuilding progressed through the centuries were the use to which the vessels were to be put, the means of propulsion, the materials available and the method of construction. As early as the fourteenth century records exist of shipbuilders using a skeleton of ribs on which planking was fixed, and at this time the stern rudder and some square rigging had already been in use for nearly a century. It can therefore be seen that the basic principles of design were established at an early stage. The refining of that design which resulted in the modern sailing ship took many centuries.

During the fifteenth and sixteenth centuries the appearance of the hulls of European vessels began to change considerably (*Figure 5*). The double-ended ship was abandoned in favour of one with a squared-off stern, and even larger 'castles' were constructed fore and aft, integrated more carefully with the hull. The triangular form of the forecastle was adopted for the bow below, the beam narrowed, and the galleon came into being (*Figure 6*). More stability was obtained by flattening the bottom of the ship, which also had the advantage of creating more space. This principle survived almost to the end of the seventeenth century.

The requirement to carry ever-increasing numbers of heavy guns resulted in the sides of vessels being sloped inwards, to improve stability by moving the centre of gravity more amidships. This also had the benefit of making it more difficult to board during battle, as the rails of two fighters lying side by side were a considerable distance apart. This slope is known as *tumblehome*, and each nationality introduced distinctive characteristics, as Figure 7 shows.

The high poop had been developed to provide a commanding position from which to sail the vessel and do battle, but towards the end of the seventeenth century the disadvan-

Figure 5 A ship of the Cinque Ports (1280). The information used in the construction of this model was drawn primarily from representations on seals of the period. The fore and after castles were temporary, erected only for fighting purposes.

Figure 7 Tumblehome. The inward slope of the sides of ships varied from nation to nation, and tended to become less as ship design progressed.

Figure 6 An Elizabethan galleon (1600). This vessel has fine lines, a forecastle set well back from the stem and a long beak, all firmly established principles at the time. A four-masted rig was normal for larger Elizabethan men-of-war. The topgallant masts and sails on the main and foremast were a recent innovation, but the square topsail at the main mizzen and bonadventure mizzen, as well as the spritsail topsail, had not yet been introduced.

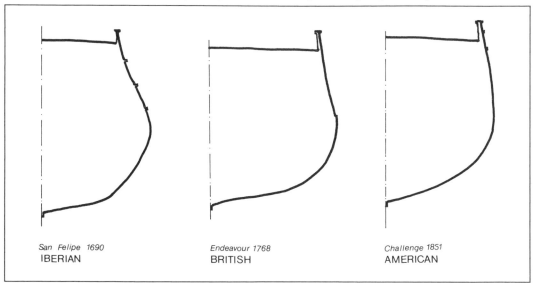

San Felipe 1690
IBERIAN

Endeavour 1768
BRITISH

Challenge 1851
AMERICAN

tage of manoeuvring the ship with the wind abeam began to outweigh other considerations. The spritsail and spritsail topsail had been introduced as a means of counterbalancing the effects of the wind on the poop, but this made it impossible to see forward, and even the provision of a lookout was not conducive to good navigation. By the mid-eighteenth century the height of the poop and superstructure generally had been considerably reduced, and during the nineteenth century these disappeared altogether. Towards the end of the seventeenth century large vessels began adopting the use of the staysail, until then used only on smaller craft. These were set on the stays between the masts, and when the spritsail topmast was discarded in the early 1700s, a new staysail called the jib was set on a jib boom rigged on the bowsprit.

The triangular lateen sail of the galleys and fishing boats of the Mediterranean was used as the mizzen on larger European ships, and retained for nearly three centuries. Not until the mid-eighteenth century did the long lateen mizzen spar give way to the shorter gaff. The small sail often found at the top of the fore- and mainmasts became a much larger topgallant sail by the mid-1600s, about which time the Dutch introduced stepped topmasts. The mid-seventeenth century saw the birth of the three-masted ship, with three sails on each of the fore- and mainmasts, and a topsail and lateen sail on the mizzen. By the 1750s the full-rigged ship had become commonplace, with the same number of sails on each mast. This term was used to describe merchantmen, as warships similarly rigged were classified by rating: ship of the line, frigate or sloop.

The mechanical revolution of the nineteenth century inevitably influenced the design of sailing vessels. Iron bands began to replace rope fittings, iron trusses were used instead of rope ones while chain replaced some of the heavier running rigging. From about 1870 British ships began to have wire standing rigging which was less expensive and far more durable than the tarred hempen rope used for centuries previously. Deadeyes and lanyards gave way to turnbuckles. Block sheaves were fitted with pulley wheels; and the general effect of all these improvements was to lighten the workload of the sailors, so that larger ships could be sailed with fewer men. Attempts to build iron ships proved highly successful, and, as steam power was already available, it was not long before this innovation was installed, at first to assist sailpower, and ultimately to usurp the long-held position of the sailing ship on the sea-routes of the world.

CHOOSING THE SCALE OF THE MODEL

In choosing a scale for a model ship, the first thing to consider is the ultimate fate of the completed work. Is it to be displayed under glass in the hall or living room? Or perhaps donated or sold to a museum or other collector? In any event, the *size* of the model is almost certain to be a major factor in arriving at a suitable scale. If it is to occupy a space 2ft long and the original vessel was 200ft long, then a scale must be chosen in which 1ft of model represents about 100ft of the original, or 1:100.

Of course, there is nothing to prevent you from building a model to any scale you wish (provided it *is* to scale). From time to time unusual scales are discovered, probably with some interesting reason behind their selection. However, if you intend to buy ready-made fittings, you will clearly have less trouble finding the correct size if you use a conventional scale.

Generally speaking, the conventional scales used for model shipbuilding are as set out in the table below:

Imperial scale	1ft of model represents	Metric approximation
¼in to 1ft (1:48)	48ft	1:50
⅛in to 1ft (1:96)	96ft	1:100
1/16in to 1ft (1:192)	192ft	1:200

The imperial scale of 1 : 60 is perhaps next in popularity; and those embarking on miniature models will need the next in the sequence above, i.e. $\frac{1}{32}$ in to 1ft.

Building to a large scale such as $\frac{1}{4}$ in to 1ft has the advantages that individual pieces making up the assembly remain fairly manageable, and a high degree of accurate detail can be incorporated. The disadvantages are the size of the completed model and the quantity of materials required.

If ambition is curbed and the next scale down is chosen ($\frac{1}{8}$ in to 1ft), then it must be remembered that this is not really half the size, as you are working in three dimensions – it would be more correct to say it is $\frac{1}{2} \times \frac{1}{2} \times \frac{1}{2} = \frac{1}{8}$ of the size, at least from the point of view of volume. This can be fully appreciated if two models are seen side by side, one of which is half the scale of the other. Proceeding to the scale of $\frac{1}{16}$ in to 1ft, it will become understood that much detail will be omitted simply because it is not visible at that scale – not so much because it is too small to model. The skilled modelmaker should be able to represent *everything* that can be seen at the scale to which he is working.

Having decided which scale is to be used, resolve firmly not to depart from it under any circumstances! Every dimension, whether it be the diameter of the lower main yard, the thickness of the forecastle rail or the width of the deck planking, will faithfully reflect the size of the original! This is not as difficult as it sounds, for once a start has been made and one gets the feel of the model as the hull takes shape, the appreciation of scale becomes almost automatic.

If you are fortunate enough to obtain a set of working plans of the model to the desired scale, much preliminary work is avoided; but more often than not it is necessary to translate your research into a usable form before a start can be made. Suggestions are made in Chapter 4 on how to go about this, and the use of the pantograph is described: an essential tool in producing, for example, body sections for the construction of the bulkheads. Once you have a set of body sections, sheer plan and half-breadth plan to the scale selected, any additional information obtained from other sources may be translated to this scale by using a simple proportional method. For example, a picture might show the lower mainmast three times the height of the distance from the waterline to the rail, and the actual height may then be determined by marking off this information on the sheer plan.

The uninitiated viewer of the completed model often has difficulty in assessing scale, and after some study may express surprise when given the actual size of the vessel. This is despite the fact that there are many scale indicators available: the height of the rail, doorways and so on, which the modeller with a little experience will seek out. It is interesting that these indicators always relate to the human figure, which is our subconscious means of assessing scale. For this reason, it is helpful to include just one figure on the completed model – perhaps the captain standing on the quarterdeck – in order to dispel immediately any doubts about scale. Of course, if this suggestion is implemented, it is just as important to have the figure correctly dressed in the uniform of the period as it is to avoid anachronism in the construction of the rest of the model.

SCRATCHBUILDING

A loose interpretation of this term would be that no part of the model has been obtained ready-made, and that the modeller himself has constructed every single item. From various writings on the subject, it seems that the second part of this definition is not altogether accurate, at least in the case of some professional modelmakers, who occasionally employ others to make parts which require for their construction special equipment not readily available. This seems not very far removed from buying from a model shop, say, hardwood deadeyes which happen to be to the correct scale. It is difficult to know where to draw the line. If one considers buying ready-cut strips of the right type of wood for the planking of the hull or deck, does this constitute a breach of the scratchbuilding code? If so, what scantling of timber would be acceptable? One could hardly have the patience to start by planting one's own oak tree!

It seems reasonable to say that scratchbuilding means that the modeller builds the whole ship himself, and that there is no suggestion of a kit of parts being used. This is not only for the greater satisfaction derived from making such a model, but also, as already stated, because the likelihood of obtaining exactly the right part to the exact scale from a model supplier is small. Most items such as deadeyes, steering wheels, canon etc. have their origin in kits, and if the manufacturer has produced these to suit, say, a 1:60 scale model, he will be unlikely to have available items for a 1:50 scale model as well. In the end, you are very fortunate to find precisely the right part for the model under construction, and when this happens there seems to be no reason why you should not take advantage of it.

There is much satisfaction to be found in discovering the means to construct items which at first sight appear beyond one's capability. For example, the doors leading below from the deck of the *Sirius* have 6in (150mm) diameter brass-framed portholes, which really seemed impossible to reproduce on the $\frac{1}{8}$in scale model. However, a piece of $\frac{1}{16}$in (1.6mm) diameter brass tube cut into thin slices and pushed into accurately-drilled holes, with a piece of clear plastic behind, solved the problem very simply and looked exactly right when complete. Ingenuity develops as you proceed, and ordinary household objects are looked at in a new light to see if they show the remotest possibility of being adapted for the model.

FINAL CONSIDERATIONS BEFORE STARTING THE MODEL

By now you are likely to have gained the impression that the model you are about to start building is going to be with you a long time before it goes finally into its glass case. It is therefore important to give due thought to where the activity is to take place. A small workshop with all the necessary tools is clearly ideal, but most people are not fortunate enough to be so equipped. It is important, however, to have somewhere where you may finish off your work for the day and leave it, secure in the knowledge that when the next day's work is commenced everything will be untouched, with nothing tidied away.

A large part of model shipbuilding can be considered not to create much mess, and therefore it is possible to set up a cradle and small toolrack on a table of appropriate size. This can simply be lifted up and put away at the end of a spell of work. This has been tried at the rigging stage, and was fairly successful in that it produced no adverse criticism, provided that the vacuum cleaner was used to pick up all the snippets of thread afterwards. The main problem was recovering small parts which were dropped, such as deadeyes and blocks, which had a habit of concealing themselves in the pile of the carpet.

The great destroyer of model ships is dust, and elsewhere the construction of a glass display case for the completed model is described. An uncovered model would have to be dusted regularly, but thorough dusting is not really possible once the rigging is complete, as much of the model becomes inaccessible. The rigging itself gradually becomes greasy and dust works its way in, slowly making the lines thicker and eventually causing rot.

It is therefore important that thought be given to the protection of the model from dust even at the construction stage. Once the basic hull has been completed, sanded and given some of its finishing coats, a padded cradle should be made and the model kept under a protective covering such as a cloth or plastic sheet. A fair amount of fine dust will be produced in the construction of spars, deck fittings etc., and it is important that this dust does not lodge permanently on the model. Models of ships look good at all stages of construction, and if long periods are likely to go by when time is not available to get on with the work, it is worth mounting it in its glass case, as this will have the benefit of simultaneously displaying and protecting the model until the work can be taken up once more.

2. Sources

This short section deals with sources from which may be obtained the plans you will need for your model and the materials necessary for its construction.

SHIPS' PLANS

The basic drawings needed will vary slightly depending on the type of construction you have chosen. For a model involving vertical sections through the hull (*see p. 29*) you will need body plan, sheer plan, stern view, deck plan, rigging plan and sail plan. Some details of deck fittings may also be required, unless these are very simple items which are shown with sufficient clarity on some of the other drawings. If a method of construction using horizontal layers has been selected (*see p. 37*) then a half breadth plan will be needed instead of the body plan.

You should first investigate the scope of your local model shop. With the growing popularity of model shipbuilding, increasing numbers of retailers are carrying stocks of good-quality ship model kits by such manufacturers as Amati, Aeropiccola, Billings, Corel, Mantua and New Maquette. Generally the set of plans provided with each kit can be purchased as a separate item, and this makes a good starting-point for the scratchbuilder. Bear in mind, though, that many of the plans

available are only conjectural, and that manufacturers do tend to adjust details to suit the range of fittings which they market. Some plans are inadequate, even failing to indicate the scale to which they have been drawn. You should therefore check the information provided very thoroughly before you decide to buy the plans, and then do some careful research on the vessel selected before you make a start on your model. Ships like the *Victory* and the *Cutty Sark* which have been preserved for posterity have been very carefully and systematically documented, making research comparatively simple. The further vessels recede into the past, however, the more likely is the information available to be questionable.

In the London area there are two model shops which carry stocks of a range of ships' plans. Both have catalogues which list not only the drawings available but also publications which may be helpful in researching your vessel. The first is Maritime Models Greenwich Ltd, 7 Nelson Road, Greenwich, London SE10. This is possibly the only shop in the United Kingdom which deals exclusively with model shipbuilding. In addition to plans by the manufacturers already mentioned, there are those by Underhill, MacGregor and Model Shipwright. A visit is recommended, as an extensive range of fittings, timbers and metals is displayed. If this is not possible, full details may be obtained by post. The other shop is The Model Shop, 6 Westminster House, Kew Road, Richmond, Surrey. This shop, while also dealing with other branches of modelmaking, has a useful range of plans and publications, catalogues for which may be obtained by visiting or by post.

If you cannot find what you want at either of these shops, then there are two major British sources of information on ships. The first is the National Maritime Museum, London SE10 9NF. This institution carries a collection of over 1,500,000 plans of ships, but not all of these are available to the eager modelmaker. To quote from their guidance leaflet:

> 'It must be emphasized that most of the plans in the collections . . . are the original builder's drawings, not specifically designed for the use of modelmaking. In some cases the condition of these plans is far from perfect, they may be obscure, badly marked, too detailed, or not detailed enough, or have pieces missing. The majority, however, are legible and complete. Plans of the eighteenth and early nineteenth century rarely show more than the lines, outlines of the decks, perhaps framing details. It is very rare to find a rigging plan for a ship built before 1840, though it is often possible to find spar dimensions and other details to make one's own reconstruction.'

Their booklet on ship's plans is out of print, and so the best means of determining what is available for your purpose is to make a visit to the Draft Room at the Museum, which must be done by appointment with the head of the Department of Ships. Failing this, it is essential, if writing, to be very specific. You must state the name, date and type of the vessel for which you require drawings. The Museum will notify you of the extent of information they have on this subject, and will quote a price for preparing copies and postage. There is usually a considerable waiting list for plans, and it will take some six weeks from the time you despatch your money before the drawings arrive. The Museum has no objection to amateurs constructing models from plans so

obtained, but stringent rules apply to publication and copyright. If you are able to visit the Museum, bear in mind that they will not permit the photographing of exhibits. You may purchase photographs, but these do not always cover every view that you might need.

The other major source of ships' plans is The Science Museum, Exhibition Road, South Kensington, London SW7 2DD. Once again, a visit to the Museum is full of interest and often fruitful. You should, in the first instance, get in touch with the Bookshop, where information can be provided on the availability of ships' plans. This smaller collection includes drawings of models which are displayed and which have been constructed in the Museum's workshops. Photography is freely permitted, so that you can obtain as many views of the model as you need to augment the plans you purchase. The Science Museum Library contains a very large collection of drawings of ships of every kind, many of which are suitable for modelmaking. A Reader's Ticket must be applied for if you wish to gain access to this collection.

MATERIALS

You will find that the various-sized timber sections in suitable types of wood for your model are generally not too easy to obtain. Fortunately, the two model shops already listed (Maritime Models Greenwich Ltd and The Model Shop at Richmond) carry supplies of these materials. Priced catalogues are available on request. A broad idea of the materials and sizes is given on p. 23. The catalogues also cover the comprehensive range of fittings stocked, including rigging cord, anchors, steering wheels, davits, cannon, deadeyes and the hundreds of components which contribute to the realism and accuracy of a model ship. Both shops provide a speedy mail-order service, and will deal promptly with your requirements. Should you have any doubts about your order, helpful staff are always willing to offer advice.

3. Tools and materials

TOOLS

There is nothing particularly unusual about model shipbuilding tools. It is likely that the enthusiast embarking upon model shipbuilding will have been attracted at some earlier stage to other branches of the modelmakers' craft, and will thus have gathered over a period a set of suitable tools. Here is a fairly comprehensive list to assist the newcomer and to remind the more experienced of what might be required. You may start with a very basic set of equipment, which will gradually grow with your enthusiasm. From time to time the need arises for some specialist tool. It can often be made, with a little ingenuity, if the investment in the real tool seems too great in relation to your interest in the hobby.

Hand tools

Small tenon saw. Hacksaw. Modelling saw rather like a small hacksaw, with a replaceable blade. Fretsaw, with a range of blades from fine to coarse, and capable of cutting both wood and metal. Stanley knife, for coarse work. Modelling knife, with a variety of curved and straight blades including a chisel blade about $\frac{3}{8}$in (10mm) wide. Scalpel and blades, size no. 3 being convenient. Wirecutters. Tinsnips. A really good pair of straight-bladed scissors about the size of nail scissors: a good test is to hold a short piece of cotton at one end only, and try to cut it a few inches away from the finger and thumb.

A set of good quality chisels – at least three: $\frac{1}{8}$in (3mm), $\frac{1}{4}$in (6mm) and $\frac{1}{2}$in (12mm), together with the essential carborundum block for keeping them sharp. A 1in (25mm) flat file, a $\frac{3}{4}$in (19mm) halfround file and a $\frac{3}{8}$in (10mm) round file. A medium sized rasp. A set of needle files, square, round, triangular and flat, preferably in a range of sizes. Tweezers with both pointed and flat ends. Long-nosed pliers. A small hammer. A set of watchmakers' screwdrivers. A centre punch.

A set of G-clamps of various sizes. A small bench vice. A pin vice. A useful clamp is available which has an arm with an adjustable crocodile clip at both ends. A box of dressmaking pins and some assorted needles. A set of drill bits, including the usual range from $\frac{1}{4}$in (6mm) down to $\frac{1}{16}$in (1.6mm), together with a selection of the numbered fine bits down to the smallest no. 75.

A plane, possibly of the Stanley Surform type. Sand- or glasspaper of several grades, including the finest flour-paper.

A measuring scale of reasonable length, preferably 12in (300mm) with divisions for the particular scale chosen. Some form of inside and outside calipers, with a vernier scale. Possibly a micrometer, if a lathe is to be used.

Figure 8 A miniature metalwork lathe being used to turn a ship's gun. Note the completed gun held in a clip and being used as a guide.

Power tools

An electric drill such as the smaller Black and Decker owned by most households is useful. Better still is a miniature electric hand drill, which usually operates from a 12-volt supply. A number of these drills are available. One marketed by Black and Decker in the Minicraft series has a useful range of accessories. A chuck is rather better than a set of collets, and plastic collets are not recommended as they wear quickly and make the centring on the drill bits difficult.

A band saw has endless uses, and, if modelling is to be taken up seriously, then you should certainly consider investing in one.

A sanding disc is important, even if it is only an attachment to your electric drill.

A small circular saw can be useful, but is by no means essential for the sizes of timber envisaged. Mechanical jigsaws and fretsaws reduce manual effort, but often at the expense of accuracy.

A miniature metalwork lathe such as the Unimat (*Figure* 8) is a quality tool of considerable accuracy, and, having made the decision and bought one, you are inclined to wonder how you managed previously. The Unimat incorporates a drill press with a graduated tilt scale, and a taper-turning attachment is one of the large number of accessories available. Nevertheless, it is possible to do some turning work without a lathe if you are prepared to be a little flexible about accuracy. The following method has been used for making a few cannon for an $\frac{1}{8}$in scale model. The shank of a brass screw was set in the chuck of an electric drill held in a horizontal drill-stand, and the screw was attacked with a series of files. To achieve a reasonable result, a cardboard template of the cannon was fixed immediately below and to one side of the work. A word of caution is necessary here, as this method probably contravenes every Safety Act ever published. Great care must be exercised, and the files must be equipped with handles in order to avoid spearing your hand.

MATERIALS

Timber

Most of the model will be constructed, appropriately, of wood – the material generally used for the original vessels. Indeed, the Navy which defended the English coastline was known as its 'wooden walls'. Through the centuries of English shipbuilding, the most widely used timber was oak, and literally whole forests existed to provide the quantities needed. A first rate ship-of-the-line required some 100,000 cu. ft (2830 cu. m) of timber, or 4000 oak trees, for its construction. The felled trees were stripped of their bark and left to mature in the open, and huge timber-yards were established near shipyards for this purpose. Elm and pine, usually for mast construction, were matured in *mast-ponds*, where timber was held below the surface of sea-water by means of low-level arches, sometimes for as long as 20 or 30 years before use.

The timber used for models is unlikely to be the same as that used for the ships they represent, simply because the scale of the grain would give an unrealistic appearance. So a selection is made from fine-grained woods which can be worked to give a good finish without too much difficulty. Stain may be used to give a more accurate representation of the original.

The most commonly-used ship-modelling timbers are available in various forms:

Strip	suitable for hull and deck planking, rails, general framing	Beech, red-dyed beech, walnut, lime (basswood), red-dyed lime, boxwood, mahogany.
Sheet	for sub-deck construction, deck superstructures etc.	Beech, lime, walnut, mahogany.
Dowel	spars	Lime, walnut.

As a rough guide to sizes, the strip material comes in lengths of 1m with thicknesses of 1mm up to 6mm and widths varying from 1mm to 10mm. The sheet sizes are 1m × 100mm with a range of thicknesses from 1mm to 10mm. You should obtain a catalogue, which gives the full range of materials and sizes available, together with current prices. The materials are supplied in metric sizes only, but if you want to make a mental conversion remember that 3mm is approximately $\frac{1}{8}$in, 25mm about 1in, and 1m about 3ft 3in.

If you are unfamiliar with wood types, you should study models to note the effect created by each variety. Decking looks both attractive and realistic in boxwood, which comes in a range of warm yellow-to-brown colours. Lime is a white wood with a very fine, straight grain;

and, if the model is lacquered rather than painted, some staining may be necessary. Mahogany is brown with darker flecks of grain and looks superb when lacquered, but is rather difficult to work.

A useful source of good, mature timber is discarded furniture, and it is worth building up a small stock of the sides of drawers and the rails of old cupboard doors, provided that these are not infested with beetle. Materials used in earlier years were of much better quality than today's.

For those parts of the model which will not be seen, such as the bulkheads, which act as the formers for the hull, resin-bonded plywood may be used. This is easy to cut with a fretsaw and will not twist out of shape. For an $\frac{1}{8}$in scale model a plywood thickness of $\frac{1}{8}$in (3mm) is sufficient.

A small timber item which is often required in quantity is a hardwood deadeye. These really are quite difficult to make satisfactorily and identical in appearance, even with the help of a lathe; and as they can be bought very cheaply, they might be one of the few items you would consider obtaining ready-made. On the other hand, blocks are much easier to make, and details of a suitable method are given later.

Metals

The two metals most frequently encountered in model shipbuilding are brass and aluminium. Brass is available from good model shops in a variety of forms: round tube, square tube, rectangular tube, solid rod, angle, channel, strip, sheet and wire, and each of these is supplied in a useful range of sizes. Aluminium comes in the form of tube and sheet. It is recommended that you obtain a catalogue of these materials from your local supplier. This will indicate availability and current prices.

Both of these metals have the properties of being reasonably easy to work and capable of taking a high-quality finish, but the surface will tarnish in time, and some protection such as clear lacquer or paint is essential. Avoid mixing the two metals, as contact between them will cause electrolytic action, resulting in corrosion. Brass rod can be turned to produce many of the deck fittings such as capstans and binnacles, and, of course, cannon on earlier vessels. Pieces of brass can be connected satisfactorily by soldering, but this cannot be done with aluminium, for which a suitable adhesive must be used. Both metals can be shaped by filing, to represent smaller deck fittings such as sheaves and mooring bollards.

Brass wire of the correct gauge is useful for tubular railings, and tinplated copper wire can also be used for very small work, but being soft it needs to be handled with some care. Its very softness makes it useful for the construction of decorative items; a very simple but effective method is to twist two strands together tightly, shape them as necessary and then to hammer them flat. The resulting ornamentation can be painted gold before it is fixed to the model.

Another less frequently used metal is copper. The use for this material which immediately springs to mind is the sheathing of the hull below the waterline. For this purpose a very thin gauge material is required – almost a foil. Plates representing 48 × 18in (1200 × 450mm) to scale are cut and fixed to the model with contact adhesive. Ready-made 'tiles' are available, but these have unrealistically-scaled rivets embossed upon them which spoil the finished appearance. It is probably best to cut your own plates and ignore the representation of fixings.

Plastics

The world of plastics seems totally alien to the modelling of ships of a bygone era. There is something about plastics which seems cheap and transitory, leading some cynics to believe that at some future date all plastics will disappear in a puff of noxious smoke! There is no doubt that, because they are man-made, plastics seem unnatural as opposed to the traditional timbers and brass associated with ship modelling; yet perhaps there is some limited use for them if one considers their advantages. Perhaps if we are prepared to use modern adhesives to hold the model together, then we should not be adamant about excluding plastics from the list of constructional materials.

Polystyrene sheet is available in several thicknesses, and it can be cut cleanly with a sharp knife. It can be permanently bent by applying gentle heat – for example, steaming at a kettle spout; and it can be joined using liquid polystyrene cement which, being a solvent, literally welds the pieces together. There are several adhesives which will bond polystyrene sheet satisfactorily to other materials, and its smooth surface takes paint extremely well.

Clear polystyrene sheet is useful as a glazing material in skylights. Paint the glazing bars and frames *before* fixing them to the polystyrene, using polystyrene cement. This material can also be used to represent the small semi-transparent panes of horn sometimes used in place of glass for windows on earlier vessels. The lead cames can be represented by carefully scoring the back of the plastic using a fairly blunt modelling knife and straightedge to give either diamond-shaped or rectangular panels. If transparency is called for, great care must be exercised in the use of the cement; but if semi-transparency is desirable, then a single wipe of the cement brush over the back of the panel will give the right effect.

Opaque white polystyrene sheet, because of its exceptionally smooth surface, can be used effectively as a facing material for some of the deck fittings, such as the sides and ends of skylights and hatches. It also produces good results when used to represent the plating of iron-hulled vessels. Strips are cut to the required width, scored to indicate vertical joints, and applied to the wooden hull using contact adhesive. If the thickness of plastic used in alternate sheets is varied, a realistic impression is given of overlapping plates.

ADHESIVES

The modelmaker before the beginning of this century did not have at his disposal the advantages of modern adhesive technology. Glues in earlier times consisted of fish-oils, boiled hooves and other evil-smelling products and had to be applied hot, making the exercise both difficult and unpleasant. Their durability was somewhat doubtful, and, as a result, even today some museums will only accept models which are both glued and pinned together. The heated glue-pot existed well into the present century, and it was not until the late 1930s that Seccotine made its appearance as the first glue which could be squeezed from a tube, with a threaded pin provided to reseal the pierced cap. Almost 20 years passed before the industry set to work with a will to produce the wide range of adhesives available today.

The adhesives to be used for modelmaking must be selected for each specific task, as a suitable multi-purpose glue is not available. All of the following have proved their suitability and reliability, and can be recommended for the purposes described. They fulfil the basic requirement of providing a secure, permanent bond, have satisfactory keeping properties and are readily available at model shops and hardware stores.

White pva adhesive

This is an excellent reasonably-priced material which will meet many of the needs of the modelmaker. It is available in a wide variety of container sizes from a few millilitres to a full litre. It is considerably more economical to buy larger-sized containers, and, provided that these are kept well sealed, the glue will remain usable for some years. It is convenient to withdraw a small amount from the bulk container for day-to-day use, and this may be kept in a small plastic hand-lotion bottle or one of the smaller adhesive containers, most of which have a useful spout. A suitable stopper must be used to prevent the glue from setting in the nozzle, and for this a brass or stainless steel nail is best.

A convenient way of using the glue is to squeeze out a thumbnail-sized blob onto a clean piece of plywood scrap, and, after resealing the container, to proceed by applying tiny quantities of the adhesive to the work with a wooden toothpick. This small quantity will stay workable for about 15 minutes, after which a skin forms and the glue should be discarded by wiping it off the plywood with a damp cloth or tissue. The toothpick applicator should also be cleaned before repeating the whole process.

White pva is suitable for all timbers, and joined wood may be worked and sanded without difficulty. The glue sets reasonably quickly, but not immediately, giving time for minor adjustments to be made. Some of the advantages of the glue are that it dries with a matt finish, small amounts of excess hardly show, and larger evidence of heavy-handedness may be wiped away with a damp cloth within 10 or 15 minutes. Because of this property of virtually disappearing when dry, the glue can be used with great advantage on rigging lines. A touch of glue on a completed knot ensures that it will not later come undone after the essential piece of spare line has been snipped away.

One example of this adhesive is Evo-Stik Wood Adhesive Resin 'W', manufactured by Evode Ltd, Stafford, England.

Epoxy resin

This adhesive is usually packed in two tubes, one containing the resin and the other a hardening agent. These have to be mixed in equal quantities immediately before use. The rapid-hardening variety of epoxy resin is the more useful as the initial set takes place in five to ten minutes. After this the work can be handled safely, although you should bear in mind that full strength is achieved only after about eight hours. It is advisable to mix only very small quantities at a time in order to avoid waste, as the material is expensive.

This adhesive is valuable in that it will readily join different materials – wood to most metals, plastics and so on – and the bond formed is virtually indestructible. Very small quantities will produce the desired result, and care must be taken not to apply more than is needed as it is impossible to clean off any excess either before or after the glue has set. Make sure that the work is ready to be glued; consider carefully how much adhesive will be required, then squeeze out the necessary amount from the two tubes side by side on a small, clean flat piece of ply waste. Recap the tubes, taking care not to interchange the two caps, and use a wooden toothpick to mix the two parts together thoroughly before applying the glue to one of the surfaces. After joining set the work aside, clamped if necessary, and immediately clean off the mixing surface and applicator with a piece of tissue, leaving them ready for next time. If you are working in a rather cold environment, beware of stringing as you move the applicator from the adhesive to the work, as the fine lines of epoxy will resist all subsequent efforts to remove them.

Two examples of this adhesive are Bostik 7 Quick Set Epoxy, manufactured by Bostik Ltd, Leicester, England, and Araldite Rapid, manufactured by CIBA-GEIGY Plastics and Additives Co., Cambridge, England.

Impact adhesive

This includes a range of rubber-based glues which can be used for a variety of purposes. The particular feature of this material is that it is applied thinly to the two surfaces to be joined and allowed to dry completely, which takes 15 minutes or so. The surfaces are then brought together and they bond firmly and permanently on contact. A firm pressure is all that is needed to bring about the bond, and no clamping is necessary.

An example is Evo-Stik Impact Adhesive, manufactured by Evode Ltd, Stafford, England.

Contact adhesive

This is very similar to the impact adhesive just described, but it overcomes the main disadvantage of that material in that the bond takes some seconds to form, so that there is an opportunity of moving the surfaces into alignment. The material is thixotropic (non-drip) and is best used for applying planking to solid hulls.

An example is Dunlop Thixofix, manufactured by Dunlop Ltd, Birmingham, England.

Cyanoacrylates

This term covers the range of single-tube glues marketed under the name of Superglues. They represent a truly remarkable step in adhesive technology, and have the property of being able to bond most materials together with unbelievable firmness; but so great is this power that all suppliers go to some lengths in warning users that they, too, can be readily bonded to their work unless sensible precautions are taken. Very small quantities are required, which is as well, for the glue is expensive; and, as no mixing is necessary, all the glue in the tube can be used without waste.

An example is Loctite Superglue 3, manufactured by Loctite UK, Welwyn Garden City, England.

4. Hull construction

This chapter gives details of two widely-used methods of building a hull: bulkhead construction and the so-called bread-and-butter construction. In addition, guidance is given on the approach to making a dockyard model. Hollowed-out and machine-carved hulls are also briefly considered. The method of laying the deck and making various hull fittings is described in detail for the particular type of hull construction selected.

In choosing the type of construction you are to use for the hull of your model, you must consider whether either of the two principal methods offers any particular advantage. Bulkhead construction produces a very light hull using relatively inexpensive materials, but neither weight nor cost should influence your choice significantly. Weight is of little relevance in a showcase display, and material cost is a tiny proportion of the value of the hundreds of hours of your time you will expend in building your model. A hollow hull will need to be fully planked, and the step-by-step growth into a three-dimensional shape involved in this method has appeal to the beginner and the experienced alike. On the other hand, if copper sheathing is to be used below the waterline, then the bread-and-butter method eliminates the need for planking as well as sheathing. This latter method, with its horizontal layer construction, lends itself well to scenic and waterline models

which are truncated a little below the waterline.

If you have been fortunate, you will have obtained a set of drawings to the right scale, and once your research has satisfied you that you have sufficient information to construct an accurate model, you can make a start. But mostly it will be necessary to produce some drawings yourself, and this is not as difficult as you might think.

The lines of a ship are the means by which the contours of the hull are determined. Three sets of information are usually required by both real and model shipbuilders (*Figure 9*).

Body plan. This is not really a plan at all but a single drawing which shows a sequence of superimposed vertical cross-sections taken through the width of the hull at chosen intervals. The sections are numbered from stern to bow and, in order to avoid a confusion of lines, those from stern to midships are marked on the left side of the body plan and those from midships to bow on the right.

Sheer plan is a side elevation of the vessel. The location of the body plan lines is shown as a series of numbered vertical lines. Also indicated on the sheer plan are horizontal *waterlines* and curved *buttock lines*.

Half breadth plan shows the buttock lines as straight lines and the waterlines become

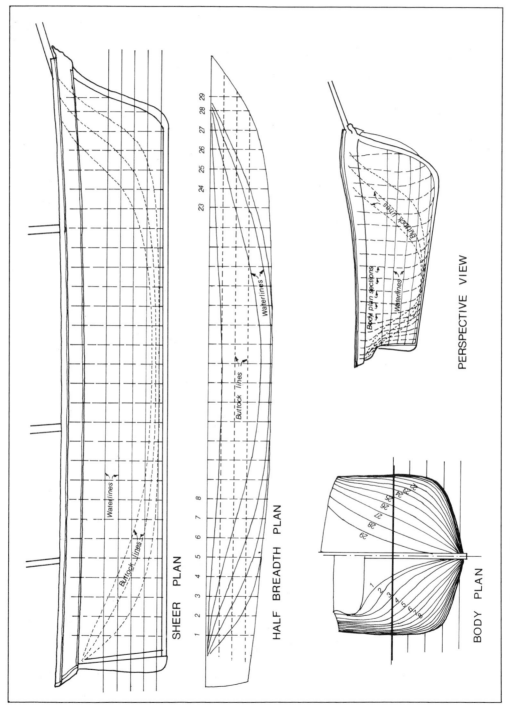

SHEER PLAN

HALF BREADTH PLAN

PERSPECTIVE VIEW

BODY PLAN

Waterlines

Buttock lines

Buttock Lines

Waterlines

Body plan sections

Buttock Lines

Waterlines

Figure 9 The three drawings which give the lines or contours of a ship's hull. The perspective drawing is included to show more clearly the meaning of the lines.

28

Figure 10 Using a pantograph to reduce the large-scale drawing on the right to the required size.

curved. A better understanding of the meaning of the lines may be obtained from the perspective view of the ship.

BULKHEAD CONSTRUCTION

Preparing the drawings for the bulkheads

First it is necessary to reproduce the body plan on a sheet of tracing paper to the scale you have chosen. This must be done with great accuracy, and perhaps the best method is to use a pantograph (*Figure 10*), a useful and not particularly expensive device which will give a large range of scale reductions. Enlargements are also possible but less successful, as the device faithfully reproduces each shake and inaccuracy to a larger scale.

The drawings for the bulkheads may now be prepared. Using the scale-converted body plan drawing and a sheet of carbon paper, trace through onto a piece of good bond paper first the centreline then the left half of section line no. 1. Now reverse the tracing paper, locate the centreline, slip the carbon paper between, and trace through the section line again to form the right-hand side of section line no. 1. Proceed with each numbered section line until you have a full set of cross-sections, remembering to mark on the deck and rail levels each time.

At this point you should decide on the thickness of hull planking and deck construction you will use, for the section lines prepared represent the *outside* of the hull, and the thickness of the covering materials will have to be deducted. A sharp ink line can then be drawn inside the lines already traced to give the size to which each bulkhead will be cut (*Figure 11*). It is also necessary to mark on each

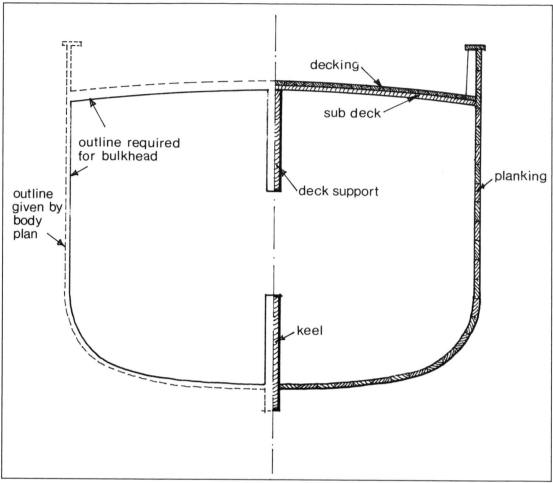

Figure 11 The left half of the drawing shows the outline required for the bulkhead, and the right side shows how the various parts of the hull covering will be added.

section a slot to receive the keel and one for the central deck support. In doing this remember that, while the keel and deck support members are horizontal, the bulkhead tops and bottoms will vary, so that the slot sizes will not be constant. Note, too, that the deck rises slightly towards the centreline to assist drainage.

Ensure that each bulkhead drawing carries its body plan number, then cut out each one, leaving a small margin all round and glue it onto a sheet of $\frac{3}{8}$in or $\frac{3}{16}$in (9 or 5 mm) plywood,

using pva glue. The reason for using good quality paper is to avoid shrinkage and cockling, and the strength of the pva glue will prevent the paper from coming adrift during the next stage. The bulkheads can now be fretsawed out, but leave the deck support and keel slots for the moment (*Figure 12*).

The keel, sternpost and stem

Refer now to the sheer plan, which will also need to be converted to the correct scale. If the

30

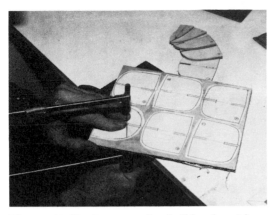

Figure 12 Cutting out the bulkheads with a fretsaw. Note that each bulkhead has been numbered.

Figure 13 The stem, keel, forward bulkheads and part of the deck support after assembly. A notch has been made in the deck support to receive the end of the bowsprit.

Figure 14 The model becomes three-dimensional. Note the doubling of the deck supports between bulkheads 3 and 4 to allow for the insertion of the foremast.

model is to $\frac{1}{8}$in scale, then a piece of lime or obeche 1in × $\frac{3}{8}$in (25mm × 9mm) can be prepared to the shape of the keel, sternpost and stem. Using carbon paper, trace the shapes from the sheer plan onto the wood before cutting them out, and use a fretsaw for the curve of the bow. A further piece becomes the longitudinal deck support, the upper surface of which will need to be shaped to the gentle curve of the deck from stem to stern. Apply pva glue to the meeting edges of the keel, sternpost and stem, and clamp the assembly onto a flat board to set.

The model becomes three-dimensional

The slots at the top and bottom of each bulkhead can now be cut so that they fit firmly over the keel, but with sufficient play to allow reassembly to be carried out a few times. Remove the keel assembly from its clamps once the glue is completely set, and, by referring to the sheer plan, mark off the bulkhead positions and numbers. Slip the bulkheads into place, and, for the first time, the model becomes three-dimensional, and some idea may be gained of the finished size and shape (*Figure 14*). Ease the deck support

31

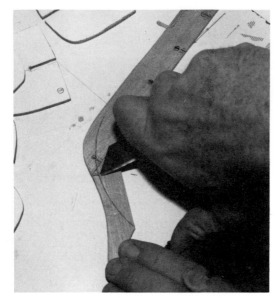

Figure 15 A groove is cut in the stem to receive the ends of the planking.

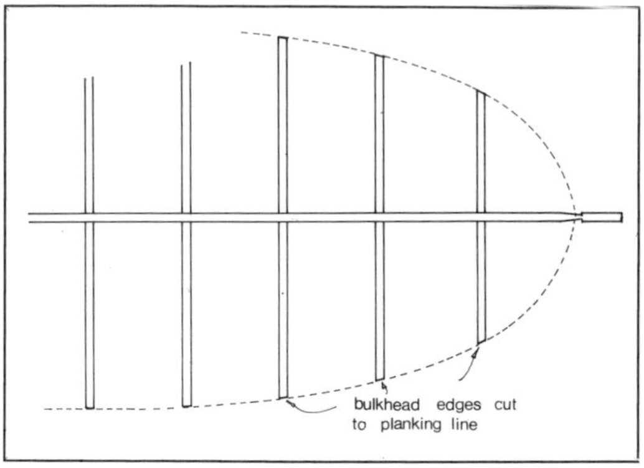

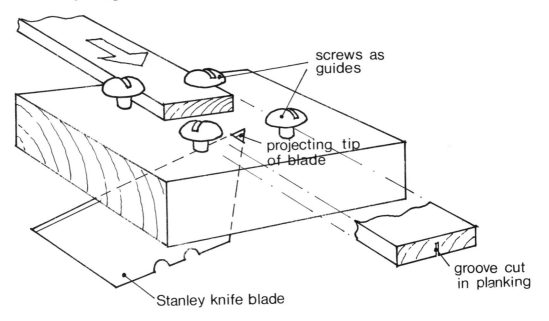

bulkhead edges cut
to planking line

Figure 16 The edges of the bulkheads need to be shaped as they approach the bow.

screws as
guides

projecting tip
of blade

groove cut
in planking

Stanley knife blade

Figure 17 A device for grooving planking. The plank is drawn through the screw guides, and the Stanley knife blade cuts a groove almost right through the plank thickness.

32

into position, and check that it lies flush with the top of each bulkhead. Mark off the position of the masts and bowsprit. Then remove the deck support, cut out the mast penetration points and form a notch for the bowsprit. Cut a curved groove in both sides of the stem to receive the ends of the planking (*Figure 15*).

Apply pva glue to the bottom slot in each bulkhead and set it in position over the keel. Next glue the upper slots and fit the deck supports, with a double piece between bulkheads to allow the masts to penetrate the deck. Glue the junctions between the deck support and sternpost and stem at either end, and, before the glue sets, pin a single strip of planking down each side of the bulkheads, to ensure that they remain at right angles to the keel assembly. Check finally that everything is square and ship-shape, and set the model aside to allow the glue to harden.

In some model kits the plywood bulkheads have short lengths extending above the line of the deck as rail posts or bulwarks, but, apart from being very fragile (if they are at all to scale), the ply edges present a poor and unrealistic appearance. If rail posts are needed, it is better to cut them from $\frac{3}{16}$in × $\frac{1}{8}$in (5mm × 3mm) limewood, splayed at the top to suit the rail width. Allow about $\frac{1}{2}$in (12mm) for fixing below the deck level, which should be marked on each post with a pencil line. Glue the rail posts in position behind the bulkheads while supporting the model in a vertical, bow-down position. Each rail post must follow exactly the profile of each bulkhead, and be precisely the right height, as it will be difficult to trim them to size at a later stage. A paper gauge may be used for this purpose.

Planking the hull

You will find that amidships the edges of the bulkheads present a satisfactory square face on which to fix the planking, but nearer the bow or stern it will be necessary to shape these edges so that they follow the line of the planking (*Figure 16*). This can be done with a medium file or a modelling knife and finished off with sandpaper, taking great care to retain the original profile. To this end, the whole edge of each bulkhead can be shaded with a felt pen or soft pencil before you start. As the shaping proceeds, the small amount of shading remaining will confirm that the original outline of the bulkhead has not been lost.

If you are working to $\frac{1}{8}$in scale, the most convenient handling size for planking is 5mm × 1.5mm. However, if you intend to reveal the planking on the finished model rather than smooth it all off and paint it, you must remember that 5mm represents about 18in, which would look unrealistic, as planking was rarely more than 9in wide. In this case, a material width of 2mm or 3mm must be chosen, or the following short cut adopted. Construct the device shown in Figure 17. The tip of a heavy-duty Stanley knife blade projects through the working surface between the screws which act as guides. Each 5mm strip is pushed through the guides until it has passed the blade, and is then drawn through in one continuous, even movement, so that a small cut, about 0.75mm deep, is made down the full length of the strip. This gives the appearance of two separate pieces, but halves the amount of work that would be involved in applying narrower planking.

The sheer plan will show where *wales* are required. These can be constructed either by using thicker planking strips or by using two thicknesses of planking, although in practice the former method is easier.

Bending the planking

There are three schools of thought on the subject of bending planking to the contours of the hull: boiling, steaming and dry-bending.

Boiling involves putting the strips into a long, inclined cylinder, about 1$\frac{1}{2}$in (37mm) in diameter, closed at the bottom and filled with water, which is boiled by applying a blow-torch. The method is sometimes used when making larger-scale models, and the object is to soften the strips, which are then applied to the model and fixed by pinning or gluing, or both.

Steaming, at its most simple, is holding the portion of the strip which has to be shaped to the spout of a boiling kettle, while applying tension in the direction of the bend.

Dry-bending is the method recommended here and is carried out as follows. A 10–15W soldering iron is required, and the shaping is done not with the soldering tip, which becomes far too hot, but with the barrel. You can either work by holding the strip in one hand and the soldering iron in the other, or can use both hands to hold the strip if you fix the handle of the iron into a pair of terry clips. Move the timber strip slowly to and fro over the hot barrel (or vice versa) a small section at a time, while applying a light stress in the direction of the required bend. Too much pressure will cause the wood to break; too slow a movement and it will blacken and burn. However, with a little practice, you will achieve good results. The strip can be bent across its length, it can be twisted and it can even be radiused to some extent; and all three of these bends will be needed for the convolutions of the hull.

It is possible to bend planking without the application of heat if a *plank bending machine* is used. This device is modestly priced, and consists of three knurled, stepped rollers mounted on a platform. The centre roller is infinitely adjustable to suit the radius of bend required. A piece of planking is fed through the rollers several times, each time adjusting the centre roller to give a progressively tighter curve, until the desired result is obtained. This machine is not capable, however, of applying a twist to the planking. This would have to be carried out afterwards using the hot soldering iron method.

Fixing the planking

The first strip is fixed at main deck level. Hold a strip against the hull and note where bends will be required. The bow curves in towards the stem, and the deck may curve upwards towards the bow and stem. Form this latter curve first, with the soldering iron fixed in its clips. Then form the bow curve. Holding the iron in one hand and with the strip face down on the bench, stroke the iron to and fro over it, lifting the stern end of the strip (*Figures 18 and 19*). As the curve forms, try the strip repeatedly against the hull until it lies snugly in position. It is important to fit the planking without any significant stress, as this could produce a twist in the hull during construction, or possibly cause planking to come adrift at some later stage.

When the first strip has been satisfactorily shaped, form a blunt chisel point at the forward end of it to fit into the groove previously cut in the stem. Then, with the model upside down near the front edge of the bench, use a wooden toothpick to apply pva glue to each bulkhead in sufficient quantity to fix just the one strip. Place the strip in position and, using a pair of long-nosed pliers, push a dressmaking pin through the strip and into the edge of each bulkhead, starting at the bow and working sternwards (*Figure 20*). Check as you go that the top of the strip aligns exactly with the top of the main deck. Cut off any excess length, allowing for the stern bulkheads which overhang beyond the sternpost and are not fitted between the keel and deck support.

Immediately fit and fix the corresponding strip on the other side of the model. Then, before the glue has set, take the final opportunity of truing-up any bulkheads which are not exactly at right angles to the keel, and of easing out any twist: after this it will be too late. Sight along the length of the model to ensure that both the keel and the deck support are perfectly straight.

Figure 18 Forming a curve in a plank by stroking it with a hot soldering iron barrel; only light pressure is needed.

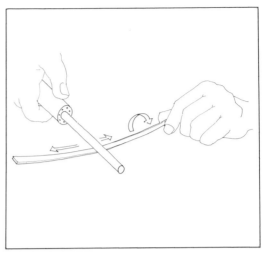

Figure 19 Forming a twist in a plank by stroking it with a hot soldering iron barrel whilst applying a twist in the desired direction. Here both a twist and a curve are being formed simultaneously.

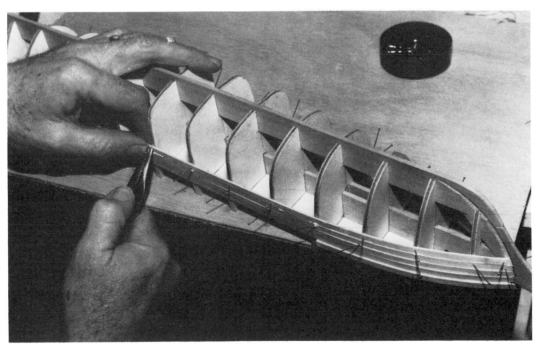

Figure 20 Pinning planking in position while the glue sets.

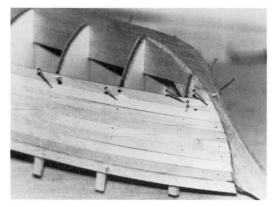

Figure 21 The pins must hold the planks tight against the bulkheads and against each other.

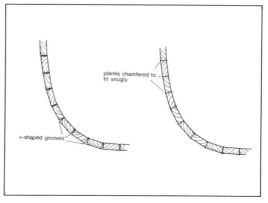

Figure 22 The edges of the planks must be chamfered where necessary in order to avoid V-shaped gaps.

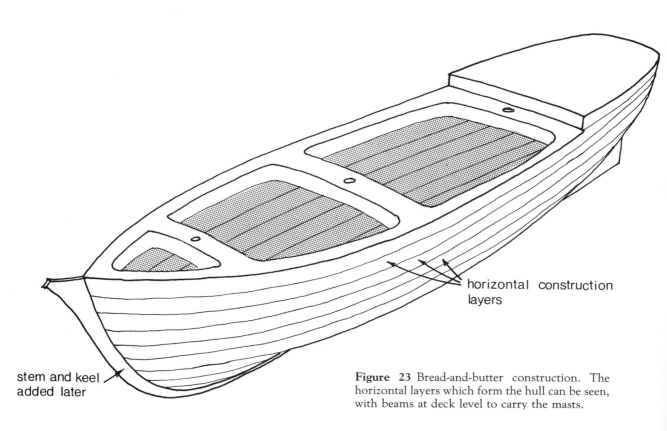

stem and keel added later

Figure 23 Bread-and-butter construction. The horizontal layers which form the hull can be seen, with beams at deck level to carry the masts.

horizontal construction layers

Proceed with the next two strips of planking, working always on alternate sides of the model and downwards towards the keel. All strips which follow the first pair must be lightly glued all the way along the top edge so that they bond not only to the bulkheads but also to each other. The pins must be pushed in in such a way that the strips are tight against the bulkheads and against the preceding strips (*Figure 21*). When three or four strips have been fixed on each side, the stern bulkheads may be glued and inserted, with careful reference to the drawings to ensure that they are located correctly.

If gunports or other openings are required in the hull, it is easier to form them at this stage rather than having to cut them out afterwards. Stop the planking on either side of each opening, bearing in mind that the sides of ports were always vertical. The head and cill of each opening can be trimmed to shape later.

As the planking proceeds you will find that the configuration of each strip becomes very complex as it twists beneath the stern. But if the model is to be accurate then you must be prepared to go on trying until each plank lies snugly in position against its fellow and the bulkheads before you glue it in position. As the glue dries the pins may be pulled out with pliers, but do not be impatient to do this. Perhaps three or four rows of pins will be in position before the first row can be removed.

Depending on the radius of the internal curve below the stern, the planking width will need to be slightly tapered near the stem and stern. This will maintain the horizontal run of planking all the way down to the keel and avoid the need to insert unrealistic, odd-shaped pieces to complete the planking. There is no set formula for making this adjustment and you must estimate the degree of taper required by thinking ahead after fixing every two or three planks. You will also notice that it is necessary to chamfer off the edges of the planks when rounding the curve leading to the keel, in order to avoid V-shaped gaps between the planks (*Figure 22*).

Planking is now complete from deck level to keel, and all that remains to be done is to apply the few remaining planks to form the bulwarks. It is worth bearing in mind at this stage that it is a great deal easier to lay and sandpaper the decking without any obstacles, and you might delay the addition of the bulwarks until the main deck is finished.

The hull must now be glasspapered using a selection of papers from medium to fine. In some places, particularly where curves are steep, the edges of planks will project slightly. Once these have been rounded off, the glasspapering action must be confined to the direction of the planking, otherwise scratchmarks will appear on the finished work. Limit your efforts to the areas which require smoothing: on no account round off corners which should remain square, or you will destroy the appearance of realism.

BREAD-AND-BUTTER CONSTRUCTION

The preparations for this method are similar to those required for bulkhead construction, in that a good set of drawings is required to the same scale as the model. In this case, however, instead of providing vertical contours by using bulkheads, horizontal layers will form the configuration of the hull (*Figure 23*). For this you will need a number of waterline sections spaced at intervals which correspond with the thickness of timber you intend to use, and, for a $\frac{1}{8}$in scale model, $\frac{1}{2}$in is an appropriate thickness. Select a material which will not warp or twist; if you use pine, ensure that it is properly matured and free from resin. Perhaps the best material is jelutong, but if this is not available you might turn to your stock of wood from discarded furniture: some $\frac{1}{2}$in drawer sides might be suitable, and joints will be acceptable provided that they are staggered in each layer.

In arriving at the outline of each layer, you must remember that, if planking is to be applied, then the thickness of that material must be deducted from the finished size. You may have decided to sheathe the hull in copper below the waterline, in which case you must form a recess in the layers from the waterline upwards to receive the planking, as it would not be necessary to plank underneath the copper (*Figure 24*).

Making the layers

Mark off the contours onto a sheet of stout paper by using tracing and carbon paper. Hold the sheets firmly in position with masking tape. Once any deductions from the outside line have been made, the cutting line can be inked in, using French curves if necessary. Then draw another line about ¾in (20mm) inside the cutting line, so that the internal part of each layer can be removed, for it serves no useful purpose. The layer immediately below deck level, however, should have 1in (25mm) wide beams left across the width of the model, through which will pass the masts. The outlines can now be numbered, cut out and glued onto the timber; and once the glue has dried, the layers themselves can be cut out using a fretsaw, or if you are mechanised, a jigsaw or bandsaw. Great care must be taken, ensuring that the blade cuts right up to the line without cutting it away – for that means starting again.

Now drill about a dozen evenly-spaced screwholes through each layer, with countersinkings on the underside for, say, ¾in (20mm) × no. 6 screws. Lay the first (deck) layer upside down on the bench and apply pva glue evenly to the surface. Place the next layer over it, ensuring that it lies precisely in position, and secure it temporarily by means of a panel pin near the bow. Check the location once again, and put in a further pin near the stern. After a final check drive in the screws, making sure that the heads go just below the surface of the wood (*Figure 25*). Proceed in a similar fashion until all the layers have been bonded and screwed together. Then put the model aside until the glue has set properly.

The steps formed by the hull layers must now be reduced to present an even sheer. It would be disastrous at this stage to remove too much material, and one way of avoiding this is to paint the stepped hull a dark colour before you start smoothing it off. You can then work with confidence knowing that as long as a thin painted line remains at the top of each layer, you have not gone beyond the original outline. The awkwardly-shaped hull may be held by one of the mast supports and rested across the knees while a surform is used for this part of the work. When you are satisfied with the rough shape of the hull, smooth it off with glasspaper, first a medium grade and working through to a fine one.

You must now turn your attention to the longitudinal curve of the main deck. You have built the hull to the maximum height, and now, by referring to the sheer plan, a number of points at regular intervals should be marked off on the hull sides, using one of the joints between layers as a horizontal datum (*Figure 26*). Join these points in a smooth even curve to indicate the amount of material to be removed, and use a Surform to cut away the wood until the correct deck line is obtained. Check from time to time for symmetry of level by placing two blocks of wood across the width of the hull, one behind the other, and sighting across them to ensure that they are parallel.

The keel, sternpost and stem

Trace the keel, sternpost and stem from the sheer plan, and then use carbon paper to transfer their outlines onto a piece of obeche of suitable width. Fretsaw the pieces out and try them against the hull. Cut and shape each piece a little at a time until it fits snugly, then apply pva glue to the meeting edges and set them in position. Use pins to hold them until the glue has set (*Figure 27*).

Planking the hull

The procedure for bending planking is described in detail in the section on hollow construction (*p. 33*). You will find that bread-and-butter construction gives a considerably

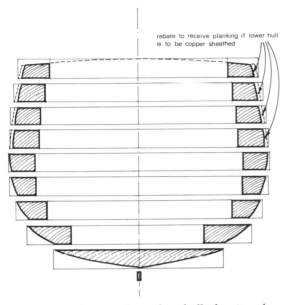

rebate to receive planking if lower hull is to be copper sheathed

Figure 24 Section through a hull showing the horizontal layers separated for clarity.

more rigid basic hull at this stage than an assembly of plywood bulkheads. This will allow a degree of spring in the planking, providing that this is not so excessive that the planks are prevented from bonding properly to the hull. In this instance, contact adhesive may be used in preference to pva glue. The bond will form more rapidly, and less pinning will be needed to hold the planks in position.

DOCKYARD MODELS

The object of the Admiralty Board dockyard model was to illustrate in every respect the vessel being proposed, not only its general shape and appearance but also its detailed construction. To this end, conventional areas of planking and decking were omitted in order to expose the substructure (*Figure 28*). Study these models carefully before deciding to

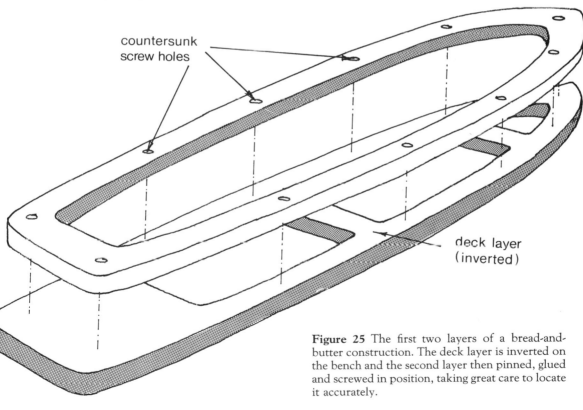

countersunk screw holes

deck layer (inverted)

Figure 25 The first two layers of a bread-and-butter construction. The deck layer is inverted on the bench and the second layer then pinned, glued and screwed in position, taking great care to locate it accurately.

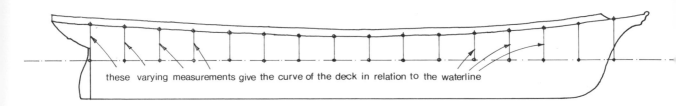

these varying measurements give the curve of the deck in relation to the waterline

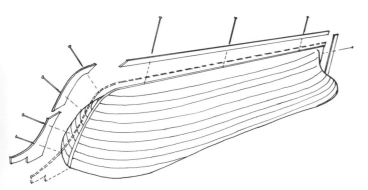

Figure 26 Method of plotting the curve of the main deck. The measurements are transferred from the drawing to the hull and marked off from a horizontal line (waterline).

Figure 27 Applying the keel, sternpost and stem. Note the flattened surface on the hull which allows these to fit squarely.

Figure 28 Dockyard model. The frames and their relation to the keel and keelson are clearly shown by the omission of planking to the lower part of the hull. The ornate decoration to the bow, stern and gunports may also be seen.

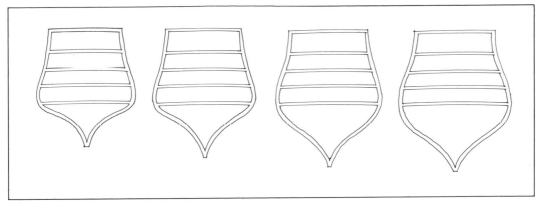

Figure 29 Drawings of four of the stern frames for a dockyard model. These would be transferred to a sheet of timber of suitable thickness and then cut out with a fretsaw.

embark on a project of this magnitude – probably the most difficult area of model sailing-ship building. Every frame will need to be individually shaped, every scarfed joint in the keel assembly represented, every member of the entire construction sized precisely to scale. And, while the parts omitted on such a model, such as planking and decking, were comparatively easy ones to represent, it was usual to include all the decorative work in full colour. Another matter to consider is whether you will be able to obtain sufficient accurate information, for of all model types surely this one needs the greatest authenticity. Your research will provide you with perhaps several useful views of the ship you intend to model, even a set of ships' plans; but how are you to be sure that internal constructional details you reveal are correct? And how would anyone know whether you were right or wrong?

Preparing the drawings for the frames

To be more positive, let us assume that you are to build a model from an existing dockyard model, and that you have photographs, plans and full documentation. The conventional scale for these models was $\frac{1}{4}$in, but of course it is not essential to use this scale if it is not convenient. Your first drawing, on tracing paper, will be a series of vertical sections through the vessel taken at each frame. Each section will show not only the outer profile but also the depth of the frame itself, as well as horizontal members such as deck beams – a true scale representation of each frame as it existed in the original vessel (*Figure 29*).

Frame construction

When all the frames have been drawn, transfer them, by means of tracing through a piece of carbon paper, onto a sheet of timber suitable for this part of the construction. This may be lime or boxwood, and its thickness should correspond with the required thickness of the frames – perhaps 3mm if you are working to $\frac{1}{8}$in scale. Ensure that each frame is numbered before embarking on the long task of fretsawing them out. When this has eventually been completed you will have a set of hollow frames ready to be linked together to form the hull.

The keel, sternpost and stem

These three members will be fully visible, and will thus have to be built up exactly in

41

accordance with your plans. The keel, floors, keelson, inner and outer sternposts, stern knee and stem timbers will all have to be modelled and assembled with authentic joints. The keel assembly will have to be slotted at the correct spacings to allow the insertion of the frames. You will see that a wealth of documentation is necessary if your model is to be anything other than conjectural.

Assembling the hull

The complexity of the construction is such that the assembly of the hull should be done in a number of sections so that access to the interior may be gained while internal fittings are installed, and only when these are complete should the sections be joined together and the wales and planking applied.

The frames are located in the slots in the keel assembly and held by wales on either side. Once this has been done, planking may be applied using one of the methods described in the section on bulkhead construction (*p. 34*). In addition to gluing the planking to the frames, brass pins are often used as a conventional feature. For larger scale models, boxwood planking pins or *drenels* may be used to give a professional appearance to the hull.

On some vessels additional strength was given to the hull by the introduction of bands of *doubling* between the frames in strategic locations (*Figure 30*). Shaping these intermediate sections of frame is not easy. One method of achieving good results is to produce a second set of complete frames for the areas where doubling occurs. The hull is assembled temporarily using both sets of frames, and the doubling bands marked on in soft pencil. The hull is then dismantled and the doubling pieces cut out, the remainder of the second set of frames then being discarded. Reassembly can then take place, and the accurately-shaped doubling glued in position using the pencil marks as guides. The hull is then ready for the application of planking, final glasspapering and finishing.

HOLLOWED-OUT HULLS

This method might also be termed the vertical bread-and-butter system. It involves producing a number of vertical sections through the model spaced at close intervals which equal the thickness of timber to be used for the construction of these sections. When cut out and clamped together these sections form a complete solid hull, which may then be glasspapered to a satisfactory finish. Before finally gluing all the sections together, separate them and remove as much as possible of the internal material. Arched beams are left in position to support the decking, and as in the dockyard model, any internal fittings which will be seen, such as gun decks, are constructed and installed. The method can be used quite satisfactorily for small scale models, and here it may be felt that the removal of the interior is unnecessary (*Figure 31*).

There are models in existence where the planking has been indicated by scoring the sides of the hull, and perhaps if this is done with great skill it is acceptable; but the appearance of real planking and wales is such that the discerning modelmaker would consider the extra effort worthwhile.

The vertical bread-and-butter method is suitable for the construction of ships' boats, and these may either be left solid with some form of canvas covering to the top, or hollowed out so that the bilge-boards and seats can be modelled. These boats were generally clinker-built, and the representation of lapped planking to such a tiny scale poses quite a problem. One way of indicating it is to glue narrow overlapping strips of paper along the sides of the boat which, when painted, give a realistic appearance.

SOLID HULLS

On the American market many kits include a ready-made machine-carved solid pine hull with reasonably accurate lines. The initial construction of this type of model is to thin

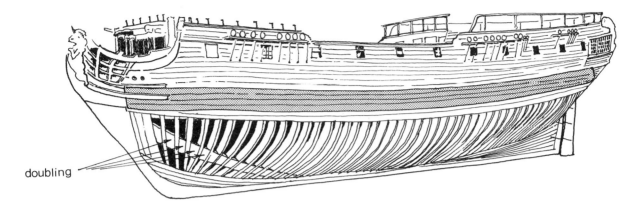

doubling

Figure 30 Dockyard model showing doubling between the frames.

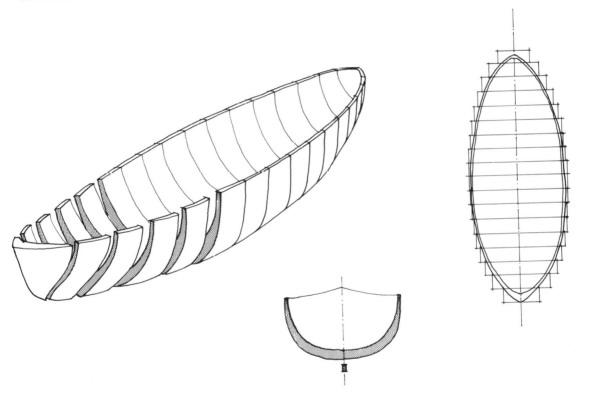

Figure 31 Hollowed out hull, showing method of setting out and construction.

down the bulwarks to the proper scale, and form a level surface on the centreline under the hull to which the keel sternpost and stem may be fixed. This is described in the section on bread-and-butter construction (*p. 37*). If a full maindeck is required, with the quarterdeck and forecastle decks above, it is necessary to cut away the solid versions of those which are provided and rebuild them with frames and planking. The hull can then be glasspapered down to a smooth surface, and planking and wales applied as described previously.

DECKS

It is possible to lay the decks directly onto the tops of the bulkheads or, in the case of bread-and-butter and hollowed-out construction, onto arched framing members across the width of the hull, as was done in the case of real sailing ships. But at $\frac{1}{8}$in scale it is convenient to lay a sub-deck across the bulkheads to carry deck fittings as well as the decking itself. This sub-deck should consist of a sheet of $\frac{1}{16}$in (1 mm) limewood or obeche, and because the deck is curved in two directions – from stem to stern as well as across the width – the sheet should be cut into four quarters. The sheet should overlap exactly half of the deck support, which is the centreline of the model (see keel, sternpost and stem under hollow construction, *p. 30*). Apply pva glue to the bulkhead tops and deck support for the first quarter of the deck, and, using long-nosed pliers, push pins through the deck sheet into the bulkheads, pressing down well to ensure that overall contact is made with the glue. Try the next adjacent sheet, and make any necessary adjustments for a good fit against the first. Mark the position of the mast fixings, then apply glue and fix as before. Fit the remaining two sheets in the same way. Check thoroughly that the deck follows the shape of the bulkhead tops, then set aside for the glue to dry (*Figure 32*).

The waste may now be cut away around the edges of the sub-deck using a modelling knife.

Avoid working against the grain, or the timber will split. Refer to the plan of the deck and mark accurately onto the sub-deck the position of any major deck fittings such as large hatches, funnel mountings or skylights, ignoring such items as the capstan, windlass, ventilators etc. If companionways leading below deck are to be modelled it is best to cut away the sub-deck at this stage so that ladders can be inserted later, but for skylights it is usually sufficient to paint a black rectangle on the sub-deck, unless the glazing is intended to permit a view through to some feature below. This raises the question of the extent to which you intend modelling the interior of the vessel, for there seems little point in expending a lot of effort on things which can never be seen once the model is complete. If, for example, gunports to a lower deck were to be left open it might be possible to see the decking on which the guns rest, so this would have to be modelled. Much depends on the scale of the model, but decisions of this nature must be made before proceeding too far.

Boxwood strip is available in a range of warm tones and this gives an excellent appearance to the deck. Walnut, too, is suitable, although this material has rather less colour variation. For an $\frac{1}{8}$in scale model strips 2mm × 1mm are appropriate, representing accurately the planking width actually used; and no single length should exceed about 75mm. Joints should be staggered in a random fashion.

Work down the full length of the deck from the centre outwards, using the joint between the sub-deck pieces as a centreline guide. Apply a thin film of pva glue to the underside of a strip and set it down on the sub-deck. Run your finger back and forth over the strip a few times until the glue has set. Each subsequent strip must be pressed firmly against the adjacent one as well as onto the sub-deck to ensure that the decking is perfectly parallel. If the strip does not adhere firmly, pull it loose, re-glue it and try again, as it will be very difficult to refix at a later stage. Stop the decking just inside the mast-holes and clean these out with

Figure 32 Sub-decks of 1mm thick obeche are laid across the bulkheads of the *Sirius*.

Figure 33 A strip of decking is laid across the width of the hull as a stop for the quarterdeck planking.

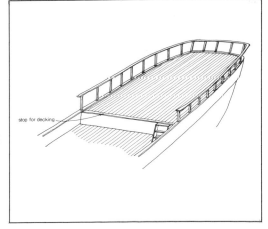

stop for decking

a round file later. Avoid exposing the end grain of strips where decks are stepped, for example, at the forecastle, by fixing a strip crosswise as a stop for the decking at the higher level (*Figure 33*).

The method described is adequate for smaller-scale models, but if you are attempting a scale larger than ⅛in, it is effective to represent the pitch joints between the deck

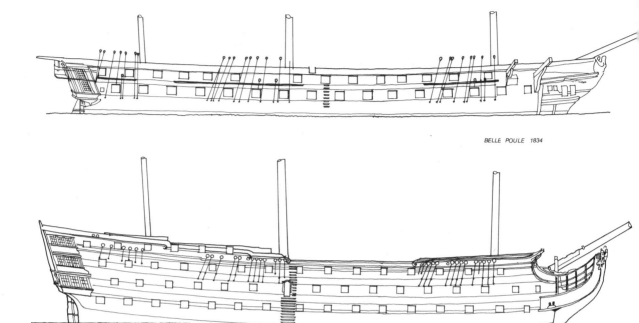

BELLE POULE 1834

H.M.S. VICTORY 1760

Figure 34 In the upper illustration, the gunports follow the lines of the planking and wales. Below, they are seen cutting across the wales, following instead the lines of the decks.

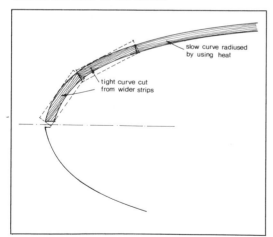

slow curve radiused by using heat

tight curve cut from wider strips

Figure 35 Constructing a tightly-curved rail by using a number of small pieces glued together.

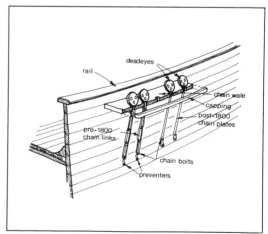

rail

deadeyes

chain wale

capping

post-1800 chain plates

pre-1800 chain links

chain bolts

preventers

Figure 36 Chain plates or chain links fitted between the chain wale and chain bolts. Note the capping piece used to hold the upper ends of the chain plates in position in their slots immediately below the deadeyes.

planks by means of narrow strips cut from a sheet of black paper using a modelling knife and straightedge. These strips are set against the edge of each deck plank immediately after laying, making use of the thin edge of excess glue which has squeezed out of the joint to secure them. It is important that the projections of black paper above the upper surface of the deck are cut away with a sharp blade before glasspapering is attempted, otherwise black dust rubs in to the surface of the decking and spoils its appearance.

Once the deck planking has been completed, the surface must be glasspapered before the finish is applied. Unless the planking is grossly uneven, you should start with a fairly fine paper and rub only in the direction of the grain to avoid scratches. Finish off with the very finest grade of paper, and apply at least two coats of clear polyurethane varnish (matt) both as a protection and to bring out the colour of the wood.

COMPLETING THE HULL

Once the deck has been finished, the bulwark planking may be applied as described for hull planking. Take particular care that the edges of the planks are glued to each other. Glasspaper the planking until you are satisfied that there is no noticeable junction between the hull and the bulwarks.

Gunports

Cut out any gunports or other openings with a sharp chisel, finally filing them to a true shape with a small square file. It is worth considering 'building-in' these openings as the planking work proceeds to save having to cut them out at a later stage; but if you do this, take care to follow accurately the sizes and spacings shown on the drawing. Gunports were parallel to the line of the deck so that the gun barrels could be located centrally in the openings, but the decklines did not necessarily follow the line of the hull planking. There are many examples of eighteenth-century vessels where gunports cut

across wales and mouldings (*Figure 34*). The head and cill members were always parallel to the deckline, while the sides followed the frames, which were at right angles to the waterlines.

Rails (caprails)

These are shaped by radiusing on a hot soldering iron as previously described, and fixed with pva glue to the top edge of the bulwarks. The edges of the rails should project slightly outside the planking and inside the rail posts. If the curve of the bow is such that the rail cannot be radiused without kinking, the rail may be made up of a number of small pieces using pva glue to connect them (*Figure 35*). Support the construction on waxed paper to prevent unwanted adhesion.

Chain wales (channels)

The purpose of these timbers was to carry the shrouds clear of the superstructure and to distribute more evenly the load of the rigging. Cut the chain wales to size and fit them accurately to the curve of the hull. Drill two or three fine holes through them widthwise, so that they can be pinned as well as glued in position. They will be subject to considerable stress, as in the case of the real vessel.

Chain plates

These consisted originally of several iron links fixed to the hull at one end, by means of a chain bolt and preventer, and passing through a notch in the chain wale to the deadeye. During the nineteenth century the chain plates became single iron bars (*Figure 36*). If not purchased ready-made, the chain plates may be formed of wire of a suitable gauge. It is important to note that the proper function of the chain plates was dependent upon each operating in line with the angle of the shroud which it supported, and, as the shrouds fanned out from the mast-top to which they were fixed, each chain plate was set at a different angle (*see Figure 72*). It is probably better to leave the attachment of chain plates until rigging is being carried out.

Masts

The lower masts may be mounted at this stage. These pass through the holes in the decking and between the beams spanning the bulkheads and rest on the keel. Check the angle of rake against the plans, and align the masts by sighting down the length of the model. If necessary, use a round file on the deck openings to obtain perfect alignment. Apply pva glue to the foot of each mast and to the point where it penetrates the deck, and set it in position, making one final alignment check before setting the model aside for the glue to set.

Bowsprit

The bowsprit is mounted through an opening in the bow bulwarks, or sometimes through a hole into the hull below deck level. Note that the bowsprit usually changed from a square section to circular near the point where it emerged from the hull (*Figure 37*). Check that both the length of the bowsprit and its angle accord with the drawings.

FINISH

You may have decided to apply two or three coats of matt polyurethane lacquer to the completed hull, allowing the quality of the timber used and the excellence of your planking skill to speak for themselves. For realism, however, it will be necessary to paint the hull; and conventionally two colours are used, one above and one below the waterline.

Once you are satisfied with the unpainted hull surface, all that should be necessary is one undercoat and one finishing coat. A good-quality oil-based paint is required, and it is important that each coat is applied to the hull very thinly, using recommended thinners if necessary. Several thick coats of paint would immediately destroy a great deal of fine detail. It may be that you are using the paint to some extent as a filler, and, if so, you must ensure that when rubbing down between coats you reduce the areas not requiring filling to the original surface.

Cradle

A temporary cradle will be needed from this point until the completed model is set on its permanent supports. Divide the overall length of the hull roughly into thirds, then use the body plan to determine the profile of the hull where the two divisions occur. Mark the lower part of these profiles onto a piece of plywood or other suitable scrap, allowing about 1in (25mm) from the keel to the bottom of the cradle. It is important that the model is supported so that the waterline is horizontal. The keel is not always parallel to the waterline, and your cradle must be constructed to take account of this factor. Fretsaw the two shapes out and connect them by means of two pieces of wood, say, $\frac{3}{4}$in × $\frac{1}{2}$in (20mm × 12mm) which are glued and pinned in place. Felt should be used to cover the surfaces of the cradle which will be in contact with the hull, in order to protect the finish.

Painting the hull

Once you have applied the undercoat, the waterline has to be marked with the model supported in its cradle. A block of wood is cut so that a pencil laid across the top of it will touch the hull precisely at the level of the waterline shown on the drawing. It is now a simple matter to move slowly round the hull, holding the pencil firmly onto the top of the block with its point against the hull (*Figure 38*).

Your research will have shown what colour the vessel was painted above the waterline, and it is likely that this would have been either black or a dull colour, as, until the nineteenth century, brighter coloured paints were very expensive, and rough sticky varnishes tended to darken quickly. Use a matt finish, or, at the

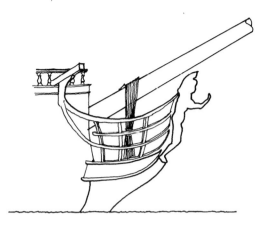

LATE EIGHTEENTH CENTURY

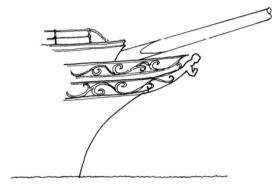

MID-NINETEENTH CENTURY

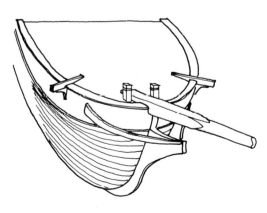

EARLY NINETEENTH CENTURY

Figure 37 Examples of variations in the construction of the bowsprit.

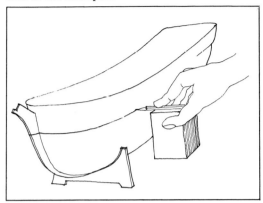

Figure 38 Marking the waterline on the hull of the model, which rests in its cradle.

very most, a satin finish paint, as glossy finishes on models always give an unrealistic appearance except in very special circumstances.

Below the waterline the finish depends on the period of the vessel being modelled. Early vessels used preservatives such as pitch and tar, and the application of these materials was effected by *careening* (*Figure 39*). The upper masts were removed, gunports battened down, stout ropes were attached to the lower mastheads, and the vessel was heeled over by barges until the keel emerged from the water. Working from rafts alongside, caulkers would remove barnacles and marine growth, burn off the old pitch and scrape bare the planking. The seams between the planks would be stopped with oakum, and the whole ship's bottom covered again with pitch and tar. The process would then be repeated for the other side of the vessel. This laborious exercise had to be carried out at regular intervals if the ship was to remain seaworthy.

Once voyages of discovery extended into warmer tropical waters, this treatment was found to be insufficient to deter the action of *teredo navalis*. This slender wood-boring

49

Figure 39 Careening a ship. The workmen, stationed on rafts, can be seen scraping off marine growth near the stern, while others apply lead-based paint after caulking the seams.

mollusc caused great havoc among the fleets of the world. One remedy was to apply a second layer of planking over the tarred and caulked hull while the vessel was careened. This detracted from efficiency, however, and of course the new surface was still susceptible to the teredo worm and marine growth.

White lead, introduced by the Dutch, was used fairly commonly from the mid-seventeenth century, and this proved rather more successful against the teredo worm than earlier treatments. However, it did little to inhibit marine growth; and if sailing efficiency was to be maintained, regular cleaning was still necessary. Towards the end of the eighteenth century copper sheathing made its appearance. Copper plates about 48in × 18in (1200 × 450mm) were fixed at first with iron bolts to the timber hull, but galvanic action soon proved the unsuitability of these fixings. Following experimental work carried out at Deptford, a new copper/zinc bolt was developed for fixing the copper sheets. For some time the Royal Navy enjoyed a twofold advantage of this new treatment. Firstly, they achieved tactical superiority, as hulls of English vessels were unhindered by marine growth and could therefore be sailed and manoeuvred more easily. Secondly, freedom from rot and attack by the teredo worm meant that ships could remain in service for far longer periods.

In the latter half of the nineteenth century, iron hulls began to make their appearance, and from their inception the most common protective treatment against rust and growth was red lead or red anti-fouling paint.

Having decided on the particular finishes and colours to be applied above and below the waterline, the means of application must be considered. It is not as difficult as you might expect to follow the pencilled waterline with a steady brush-stroke if the hull is held across the knees and you take your time. If you have some doubts as to your capability of producing a crisp, even junction between the two colours, then masking tape can be used. Alternatively, you might consider using spray painting, which can produce excellent results. There are a number of suitable matt colours available in aerosol spray cans, and one which gives an authentic representation is the red oxide used for undercoating car body repairs. Masking tape, which has the property of being stretchable on a bowl shape, is essential in this case, and you must ensure that the rest of the model is completely screened from the spray by tucking sheets of newspaper under the edge of the masking tape before pressing it down.

Decorative hull lines

Many vessels carry one or more painted lines running the full length of the hull. These present quite a problem to the modelmaker. Painting an even line by hand using a fine brush requires a very high degree of steadiness and skill. Masking tape may be a solution, and if you use this method the paint should be sprayed on rather than applied by brush. If a pair of lines close together is required, you may find it difficult to mask between them successfully. One satisfactory method is to obtain a small reel of Letraline (marketed by Letraset) of appropriate width and colour. This material is a fine self-adhesive tape available in a range of widths down to 0.4mm. It is applied simply by drawing a strip from the reel and pressing it against the hull. The straight, even line so achieved gives a professional finishing touch. It is important to use a line with a matt finish. Often the line required is gold, and this happens to be the one colour which is only available in gloss. However, if a dozen strips 8in (200mm) long are withdrawn from the reel and stuck down temporarily onto a surface such as wax paper, a matt gold finish can be sprayed on from an aerosol can. When the paint has dried, the strips can be lifted and applied to the hull. A matt varnish spray will help to secure the strips permanently.

5. Fixtures and fittings

Fixtures to the hull and fittings on the deck must be considered before you proceed with the rigging of the model, as once the shrouds and stays are in place it will be difficult to gain free access to the deck. The robust hull as it stands will become a considerably more fragile model as the yards and rigging are added, and indeed, this latter exercise will need to be carried out with the model firmly seated in its cradle.

THE STERN

Fortunately for the modelmaker who has chosen to consider only the eighteenth and nineteenth centuries, the excessive and unnecessary stern decoration of earlier years gradually died out during this period, giving way to more efficient, simple design. There are examples of vessels in the latter part of the seventeenth century which had become unbelievably cumbersome after the application of this decorative work. Captains found it necessary, once they were out of sight of land, to give orders to cut away the heavy carvings and galleries to make the vessels more seaworthy.

Before starting on work to the stern, you will find it helpful to make a scale drawing showing all you intend to model. After that it is a matter of working away with small pieces of lime bent to shape over a hot soldering iron, carrying out as much of the tiny carving as you are able with a small modelling knife, and using your ingenuity in representing the various mouldings. A lathe can be very useful. In return for suffering in silence your dentist may be prepared to give you a selection of *burrs*, which, mounted in the chuck of your miniature drill, are an excellent means of doing small-scale carving (*Figure 40*). Pieces of copper wire twisted together, shaped and hammered flat, produce some quite effective mouldings. In desperation you may resort to your model shop, where a range of decorative castings will be available. Symmetry was always important in stern decoration and you must exercise some care in achieving this, or your model will seem lop-sided even to an inexperienced observer. The name of the vessel sometimes appeared amidst the stern ornamentation, although in earlier years, when most people were illiterate, a representational carving usually sufficed.

The rudder

The centrally-placed rudder is found immediately below the overhanging stern. This was not always the case, for in Viking times a steering oar was fixed on the starboard or *steerboard* side. Earlier Roman merchant vessels carried two independently-operated steer-

Figure 40 Using a dentist's burr in the chuck of a miniature electric drill to carve the stern decorations on the *San Felipe*.

ing oars, one on each side of the stern. It was not until the Middle Ages that small ships began to use the simple and efficient rudder we know today, which was operated by a *tiller*. During the sixteenth century the stern was built so high that some mechanical means of operating the tiller remotely was needed, and the *whipstaff* came into being. This was a long vertical pole passing through the deck and connected by means of an iron band to the tiller (*Figure 41*). It can be appreciated that this allowed only a limited amount of movement of the rudder, but this was not considered a serious drawback, as the rudder was secondary to the sail in controlling the direction of the vessel. It was not until the end of the seventeenth century that the principle was adopted of moving the tiller by means of a rope wound round a drum connected to a steering wheel (*Figure 42*). This idea passed through many stages of development, but the basic principle is retained today. The entire steering mechanism (not just the ship's wheel) is known as the *helm* and is composed of rudder, tiller and steering wheel.

The rudder has a number of horizontal *pintle straps* fixed to it, and these project forward and grip the downward-facing *pintles*. Each pintle rests in a *gudgeon strap*, which is fixed to the sternpost and shaped, where necessary, to the curve of the stern timbers (*Figure 43*). The rudder, being of wood, was known on occasion to float free in a heavy swell; and to aid recovery, *preventer chains* were attached and fixed to the hull on either side. These chains could also be lashed to ropes in order to provide a crude form of steering should the tiller become inoperative.

The gudgeon and pintle straps can be made from this sheet brass, and a brass wire pintle soldered or epoxy-glued in position. Up until the mid-nineteenth century the meeting surfaces of the rudderpost and sternpost were flat. Later these were rounded to allow easier movement, and the pintle became a separate nut-and-bolt arrangement rather than being fixed to the pintle strap.

THE BOW

By the eighteenth century the bow of the sailing ship had undergone similar progressive changes to those made on the stern. The long beak had been considerably shortened, and instead of the cutwater being almost a separate construction rather tenuously joined to the stem, it became an integral part of this structure. The degree of decoration was reduced and the head timbers were raised, the whole structure thus becoming less likely to ship water in heavy seas.

Head structure

The *main rails* curve gently in two directions, and will need some care in construction. You may find it easier to piece them together than to carve them from a single piece of wood. Remember that a pair is required, and you will find symmetry easier to achieve if both rails are worked on simultaneously. The *cheeks* can be added afterwards, as these much thinner pieces can be shaped using heat in the usual manner before gluing and fixing. You might find it easier to paint or stick on any gilt decorative patterns before the main rails are fitted. A pair of *hawse holes* will be required on either side of the bow, with a *bolster* beneath each pair to take the strain and wear of the anchor rope (*Figure 44*).

The *head rails* and *head timbers*, particularly in earlier times, were curved dramatically. Although relatively thin in section, you might find them difficult to form from a single piece, in which case piecing together will again be necessary. On the upper surface of the head structure are the *knightheads* between which the bowsprit passed, as well as some planking and gratings (*Figure 45*). This space provided the crew with rather rudimentary toilet facilities, and was strategically placed, being both to leeward and frequently washed by heavy seas. The word 'heads' is still retained today in describing the crew's toilet accommodation.

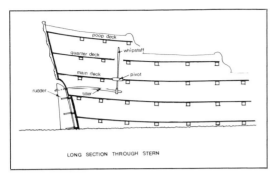

Figure 41 The whipstaff on the quarterdeck operates a tiller below the main deck, imparting a small
amount of movement to the rudder.

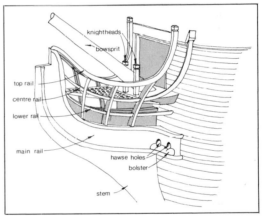

Figure 42 A ship's helm. The movement of the
ropes can be traced to show that the ship will turn in
the direction in which the steering wheel is rotated.

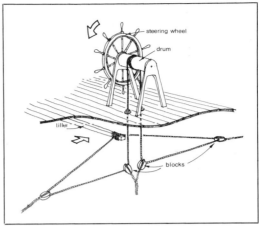

Figure 44 Bow of a mid-eighteenth-century vessel,
showing the head structure.

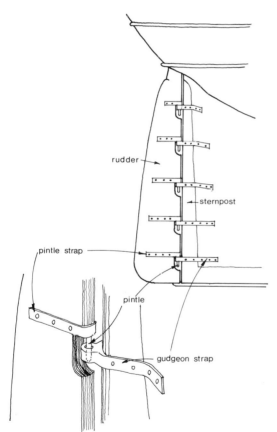

Figure 43 Construction of a ship's rudder.

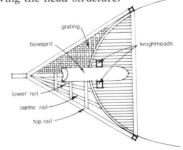

Figure 45 Plan view of the bow shown in Figure
44.

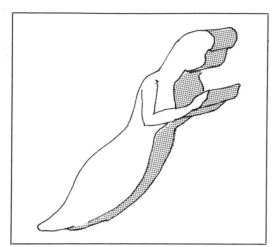

Figure 46 Carving a figurehead. The shape should be cut out in profile first before attempting to add the third dimension detailing.

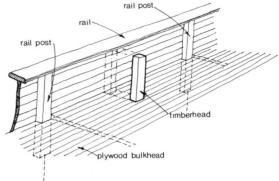

Figure 47 Construction of the bulwarks, showing how timberheads may be added between the rail posts.

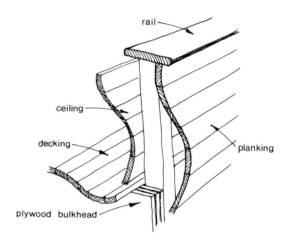

Figure 48 Section through bulwarks showing the addition of internal planking called ceiling.

Figurehead

At the peak of the junction of the cutwater and main rails a recess is formed to take the figurehead. This was usually designed in such a way as to give a continuous sweep of line to the bow structure. You must refer to your ship's plans for the figurehead required, as this varied from simple scrollwork to elaborate carvings of heraldic beasts and human figures. If the figure is human it would nearly always be female, just as ships, if named after people, nearly always had female names. Whatever the creature depicted, its eyes were to look out over the horizon and not downwards, for that would surely be the ultimate direction the ship and her crew would take.

You might try carving the figurehead from a fine-grained piece of hardwood, with a reasonable length of waste to hold it secure while you work on it. Another method is to use Plastic Padding (made by Ab. Hisingeplast, Göteborg, Sweden) or any similar resin/hardener compound used for car body repair. Cast a lump of the mixture on a toothpick and twist it in front of a heat source until it sets. When cured, the carving may be carried out using a miniature drill with the dentist's burrs mentioned previously. Always carve the figure in profile first, afterwards adding the third dimension and detailing in the round (*Figure 46*). Paint the figurehead before mounting it in position, and ensure that it is clear of the bowsprit above and does not touch the bobstay chain below.

THE DECK

Bulwarks

The construction of the bulwarks has already been described in the section on hulls, but your plans might call for additional *timberheads* which are the extension of some of the hull frames. These are cut to the correct length from a suitable section of lime, each with its head and foot trimmed to the angles of the deck and rail. Set the timberheads in position with pva glue (*Figure 47*). Sometimes ships-of-the-line had the timberheads closed off with internal planking called *ceiling* which provided an extra obstruction to cannon shot (*Figure 48*). Often this inner lining or the inner face of the bulwarks was painted a maroon/red colour.

Kevels (*Figure 49*)

Found on vessels before the nineteenth century, these horn-shaped fittings were arranged in pairs on the inside of the bulwarks and fixed through heavy horizontal timbers. Their purpose was a fastening-point for the fore and main sheets. A variety of kevels was used, some horizontal with a fixing at each end used to tie the lifts, others vertical and used singly, such as those for the cathead tackle.

Pinrails (*Figure 50*)

These horizontal fittings were fixed inside the bulwarks, projecting beyond the inner line of the rail. Cut them to shape and drill holes to receive *belaying pins* before gluing in position. Make tight joints against the timberheads, as they will be subjected to a fair amount of strain when the rigging is added.

Ports (*Figure 51*)

You will already have formed any ports required in the bulkheads as described in the chapter on hulls. At this point lids are to be added, either open or closed. Gunport lids

Figure 49 A range of kevels found on nineteenth-century ships.

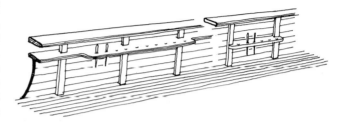

Figure 50 Two types of pinrail. The diagram on the left shows a topgallant rail over the main rail, the latter incorporating the pinrail. This system was sometimes found on merchant vessels in the nineteenth century. The diagram on the right is the type of pinrail most often encountered on merchantmen and warships of the eighteenth and nineteenth centuries.

Figure 51 The diagrams show, from left to right, a washport, side-hinged gunport, top-hinged gunport in two leaves, and a top-hinged single-leaf gunport. The latter is probably the most common form.

were hinged at the top, or split into two and fitted with side hinges. In either case the lids were held open by a line fastened to them and taken through holes in the planking to be tied internally. A simple way of making the hinges is to hammer flat a thin piece of brass wire to give the desired width; cut it to the required length and fix to the lids with epoxy glue. *Washports* were top-hinged but had no fastening. They opened to allow water on the deck to run away freely, and closed against incoming seas. *Ventilation ports* were provided on later vessels where some thought had been given to make the accommodation for crew or passengers marginally more comfortable. They followed a similar pattern to gunport lids.

Iron railings

In the second half of the nineteenth century iron railings were frequently seen around the forecastle, where perhaps the designers had felt that a raised solid bulwark would spoil the graceful sweep of the main deck rail. They were found in other locations too, such as around the paddle housing and raised centre deck on paddle steamers. If you intend to model this feature, great attention must be paid to scale: a 2in (50mm) stanchion and rail would be $\frac{1}{48}$in (0.5mm) in diameter to $\frac{1}{8}$in scale. Coarse-looking railings can quickly destroy the impression given by an otherwise carefully constructed model.

Cut appropriate lengths of stanchion from brass or tinned copper wire with a pair of wire snips. This action makes a flattening on the wire at the point of cut which must be restored to circular section with a few strokes of a fine-toothed file. Use a paper gauge to cut each length exactly. Now drill holes in the decking to receive the stanchions at the specified spacings. Make sure that the holes are vertical and that they will allow the stanchions to fit tightly. Holding each stanchion with a pair of tweezers, tap it into a hole, using a paper gauge to check the exact height above the decking. It should not be necessary to use an adhesive if the holes have been correctly sized. Apply a dot of solder to the tip of each stanchion. Keep your soldering iron clean by frequent wiping with a piece of cloth, as any excess will be impossible to remove later. Now cut a length of rail from the same wire, making it slightly longer than needed. Holding the rail in position, apply heat simultaneously to the tip of the stanchion and the rail until a solder joint is formed. It is easier not to start at one end, but do make sure that the free end is correctly located. It is not too important to get the stanchions vertical at this stage. Once you have made all the joints, any truing-up can be done by holding the offending stanchion with a pair of tweezers and applying heat to the joint. As the solder melts, the stanchion may be moved into the correct position.

The exercise described above is not particularly difficult. However, if your model calls for an intermediate rail as well as a top rail, your skill and patience will be tried to the limit. Each individual section of intermediate rail has to be cut to fit between the stanchions, solder has to be applied to each end and the correct fixing height judged without the use of a paper gauge, as both hands are occupied. The operation has to be carried out with sufficient speed to avoid the heat of the iron travelling along the wire and melting previously completed joints. Final adjustments are unbelievably frustrating, as good joints spring open in preference to those you are attempting to resolder! Cast brass stanchions with spherical socket joints are available at model shops to several different scales, and look realistic when properly fitted.

Catheads (*Figure 52*)

These two heavy timbers projected over the bow at deck level on either side and are firmly secured into the deck. They are provided with sheaves at the outer end through which pass the tackle used to raise the anchors clear of the bow. The anchors are afterwards hauled up and secured horizontally to the sides of the ship. Sometimes additional support was given to the cathead by extending the head rail so that it curved up and turned out to follow the angle of the cathead. On smaller vessels the cathead sometimes projected at rail rather than deck level, entailing a shaped member which turned down into the deck to be secured to the hull framing. The outer ends of

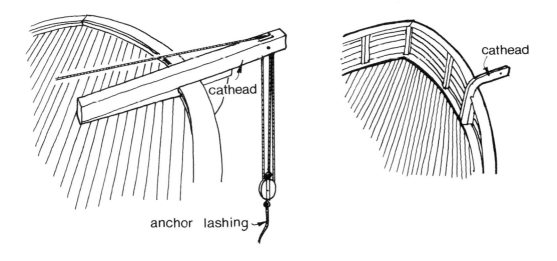

anchor lashing

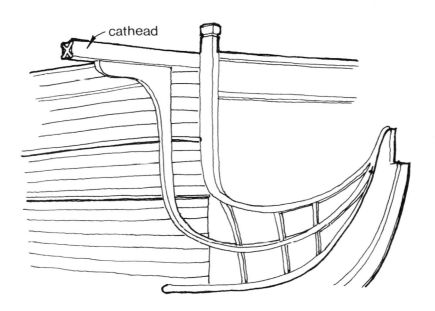

Figure 52 Catheads. The lower drawing shows the elaborate support for the cathead sometimes found on vessels of the mid-eighteenth century.

the catheads were usually decorated with some form of carving.

Anchors (*Figure 53*)

The shape of anchors changed with their development during the centuries, but the basic components remained in one form or another. Although a range of anchors is usually available in model shops, you will find it is not a particularly difficult item to make for yourself. Select a suitably thick piece of flat aluminium, which is rather softer than brass for this sort of work. Mark the outline of the anchor on masking tape which has been stuck to the surface, and fretsaw it out. Ignore the *flukes* at this stage, and file the *arms, crown* and *shank* to the required profile. Drill the eye to take the *anchor ring*. Now cut and file the flukes to shape from thinner sheet aluminium and attach them to the arms with epoxy resin or multi-bond adhesive. Paint the metalwork matt black. Now cut the *stock*, which is halved lengthwise, from a piece of lime, filing a square hole for the shank and tapering it towards the ends. Fit the stock to the shank after applying pva glue to the meeting faces. Form two or three *hoops* on either side of the stock by binding with thread or black paper strips to represent rope lashings or iron hoops. Make a wire ring to fit through the hole in the shank, attach the end of the anchor chain and close the ring with a solder joint. Bear in mind that chain was not commonly used until the second half of the nineteenth century, simply because the weight of two complete anchor chains plus a certain amount of spare would have formed an impossible proportion of the vessel's burden.

Windlass (*Figure 54*)

On smaller vessels the windlass was the usual means of hauling in the anchor-hawse. It consisted of a horizontal roller or *barrel* tapered towards the ends where it was held between two bitts. Square *bar holes* in the barrel allowed two or more bars to be inserted

to obtain sufficient purchase to turn the barrel, the bars being withdrawn and reinserted alternately as the movement proceeded. The barrel was prevented from turning back by one or two *pawls* operating in a ratchet, the pawls being suspended from a *pawl bitt*. The anchor hawse emerged from the *hawse pipes* and was looped two or three times about the windlass barrel before being led through a hatch into the *cable tier* below.

Capstan (*Figure 55*)

The capstan, too, served as a means of hauling in the anchor hawse on larger vessels. It was a vertical drum with shaped sides on a bearing fastened to the deck. Like the windlass it had square bar holes around the circumference of the cap. Several capstan bars, at first wood, later iron, would be inserted into these holes so that the capstan could be pushed round by the crew. When weighing anchor, an endless rope called a *messenger* was looped around the capstan and taken forward. The anchor hawse would then be attached to the messenger by three or four short lengths of line called *nippers*. As the upper end of the hawse disappeared into the cable tier, the first nipper would be removed by a boy who would then run forward and fasten it to the next section of hawse being drawn in. He would just have time then to run back to undo the second nipper, which would be taken forward and tied to the forward end of the hawse, and so on. It was slow work, and in deep water it might take some two hours to weigh anchor.

The main work of the capstan, however, was handling heavy mooring lines and running rigging. It would be placed in the most convenient position to serve this purpose, vessels often being equipped with more than one, the only limitation being the surrounding space required for the crew who manned it.

Fife rail (*Figure 56*)

Running rigging was secured by belaying to various points about the deck of the vessel.

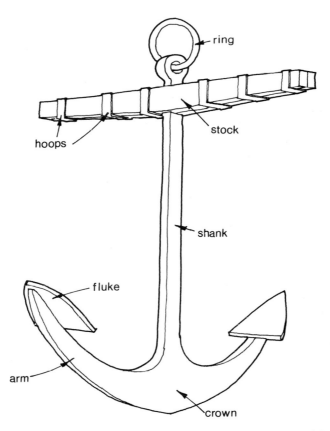

Figure 53 A common anchor. Note that the stock is made in two pieces which are brought together over the square shank and bound by means of hoops or rope lashings.

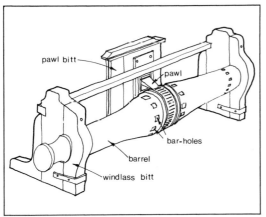

Figure 54 A windlass, showing the pawl which ensures that the barrel can turn in one direction only.

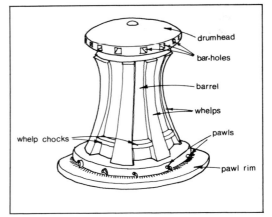

Figure 55 A capstan. In a similar way to the windlass, the pawls engage on the pawl rim to ensure that the barrel turns in one direction only.

Figure 56 The forecastle of the *San Felipe* showing the fife rail at the base of the foremast.

Around the base of each mast was an iron *spider hoop* pierced with a number of holes through which belaying pins could be thrust (*Figure 57*). The rails were sometimes similarly pierced in suitable locations, or pin rails below the rails were used. Standing close to the base of each mast was a fife rail, either straight or U-shaped, supported on decorative posts. Its flat top was pierced to receive the appropriate number of belaying pins. This item, as in the case of the real thing, requires secure fixing, and you should drill the feet of the posts and force in a pin leaving, say, $\frac{1}{4}$in (6mm) projecting. This is then pushed into the deck after applying epoxy resin glue to the feet.

Belaying pins

To ⅛in scale you will require belaying pins 3/16in (5mm) long with a maximum diameter of 1mm. The feasibility of turning such a small piece of brass wire even on a miniature lathe is doubtful. You must also bear in mind that a fair number of them will be needed. Well-made belaying pins in brass with properly shaped heads and tapered shanks are available quite cheaply at model shops, and in this instance are probably the best solution. To larger scales, belaying pins turned in boxwood are available, or perhaps it would not be too unreasonable to try your hand at making these.

Hatches (*Figure 58*)

On earlier vessels, hatches were simply covered with some form of wooden trap. In time the need for ventilation brought about the introduction of *gratings*. The hatch *coaming* was sufficient to deflect moderate washes of rough sea, but in heavier weather the gratings were covered with tarpaulins lashed to eyes around the coaming. Gratings can be bought ready-made or as kits of slotted

Figure 57 A spider hoop fitted near the base of the mast, to which running rigging may be attached.

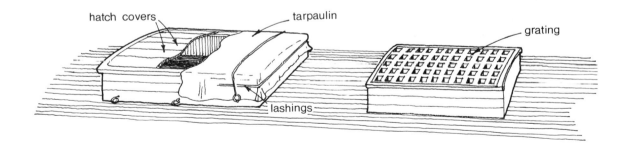

Figure 58 Two types of hatch. The earlier version is shown on the left, with a tarpaulin cover lashed over it and fixed to eyes in the coaming.

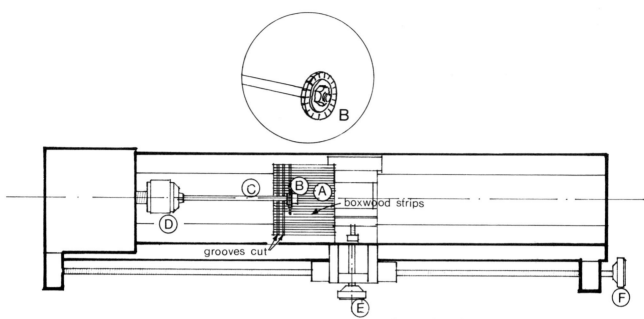

Figure 59 Plan view of a miniature lathe showing how it might be set up to produce slotted strips from which a grating could be assembled. Inset is a view of a small sawblade made by cutting slots around a metal washer.

strips which can be fitted together egg-crate fashion. If you have the equipment, you might try making your own (*Figure 59*).

Cut a number of 3in (75mm) lengths from 2mm × 1mm boxwood strip. Lay these together side by side, narrow face up, on a flat bed of 3mm sheet. Clamp them firmly together with a piece of 3mm × 2mm strip on either side glued to the bed. Clamp the whole assembly into the jaws of a machine vice fixed to the carriage of a miniature lathe (A). A very small circular saw blade is required, and for this purpose a simple one can be made by using a hacksaw to cut a number of slots around the rim of a ⅝in (15mm) diameter metal washer (B). Fix the washer into some form of arbor about 3in (75mm) long (C), and set it into a drill chuck on the drive spindle of the lathe (D). Position the longitudinal slide so that the boxwood assembly is in line with the blade. Now set the lathe running, and operate the cross slide (E) so that the assembly moves

below the blade, cutting a groove right across the boxwood strips. After a few trials and adjustments you will be able to make a groove 1mm wide and 1mm deep. The carriage is then moved 3mm along by observing the graduations on the handwheel (F), and the next groove cut. When all the grooves have been made, remove the boxwood strips, cut them to the required length, apply pva glue inside the grooves and assemble the grating.

At the sides of the gratings on warships were fitted racks where cannon shot could conveniently be held ready for action. These racks were known as *garlands*, or on some English vessels as *monkeys*. On more ornate ships these were sometimes fashioned in brass. This was not a particularly successful material, as water in the sockets would invariably freeze in winter, dislodging the cannon balls. This may have been the origin of the expression sometimes used to describe the severity of cold weather.

64

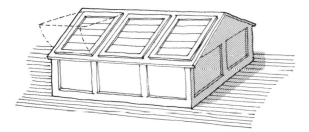

Skylights (*Figure 60*)

During the early part of the eighteenth century, fixed skylights were fitted in the poop deck, the glazing giving the steersman at the whipstaff an opportunity of seeing the set of the sails. In later years skylights were provided with sloping covers which could be opened to assist ventilation, and they were deployed in greater numbers about the deck.

Cannon

Ships' guns warrant a special study of their own. It is recommended that you research the period of the vessel you are modelling in this

Figure 60 A glazed skylight. The upper sloping sections could be propped open if required, and the glass was protected to some extent by means of iron bars fixed across them.

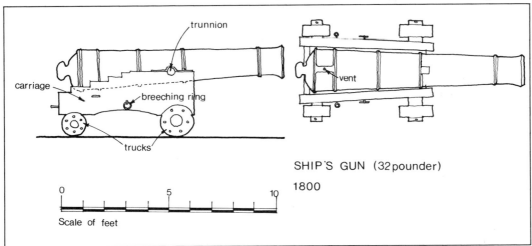

trunnion

carriage

breeching ring

trucks

vent

SHIP'S GUN (32 pounder)

1800

0   5   10

Scale of feet

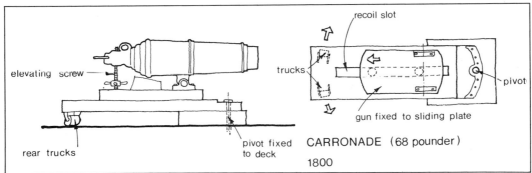

recoil slot

elevating screw

trucks

rear trucks

pivot fixed to deck

gun fixed to sliding plate

pivot

CARRONADE (68 pounder)

1800

Figure 61A A 32-pounder ship's gun. The scale will enable you to model the gun with accuracy.

Figure 61B A 68-pounder carronade. The gun and its bearing plate moved in the recoil slot when fired or being run out.

respect to be reasonably sure of the authenticity of the guns you intend to show. Cannon are, of course, available in model shops, but the difficulty is getting the right ones to the right scale. Figure 61 shows two types of gun and a *carronade*. The former sat on a carriage with four *trucks* (wheels). They were run out before firing, the recoil driving them back to the extent of the *breeching rope*. The carronade, on the other hand, was a lighter weapon, and the front of the carriage was pivoted to the gun deck, with two trucks at the rear to permit aiming. A greased *bearing plate* on a *slide* enabled the gun to be run out and allowed for the recoil.

This is one of the easier exercises to carry out on a lathe, and great satisfaction can be gained from comparatively little effort and expertise. Use brass rod of economical diameter, and some form of template to ensure that the guns are identical. The carriages are made up of three pieces of mahogany or dyed beech glued together with pva adhesive. Short sections of $\frac{1}{8}$in (3mm) dowel or brass rod will serve as trucks.

Ship's bell

Most vessels of any size possessed a bell, which was the means of marking the passage of time. An hour-glass designed to measure half hours was kept running before the helmsman and each time the sand ran out he was required to turn over the glass and ring on the bell the number of half-hours elapsed. Each watch was divided into four hours, or eight *glasses*, and eight bells denoted the end of each watch. There were six four-hour watches in a 24-hour period. On larger vessels the number of glasses was repeated by the lookout who was stationed at the main bell. For ease of counting, bell-strokes were always made in pairs, with odd strokes at the end.

The means of housing the bell varied from a simple iron frame to a decorative belfry such as may be seen on Nelson's *Victory*. The bell itself is another opportunity for the lathe enthusiast to show his talent.

Davits (*Figure 62*)

In medieval times ships usually towed their boats and barges. In later times they were hung from timber davits fixed to the side rail caps at the stern, or projecting at an angle outside the bulwarks. Boats were commonly stowed inverted over a pair of skids fitted across the deck, conveniently located so that they could be slid overboard when required. From the mid-nineteenth century, davits were constructed of iron and fixed to the deck, curving outwards to suspend the boats clear of the bulwarks. This system enabled the boats to be manned before lowering, and was the forerunner of the modern lifeboat.

FITTINGS ON STEAM-ASSISTED VESSELS

The late 1830s saw the arrival of vessels powered by both wind and steam, and this brought about many changes in the layout of the decks. While the windlass was sometimes retained, the manually-operated capstan disappeared, for much less space-consuming steam winches could be used. These were often located out of sight below deck. More skylights appeared as accommodation for both crew and passengers improved. Hatches to coal bunkers were needed, and companionways leading below were numerous. Above all this stood the funnel, usually with one or two whistle-pipes accenting this intrusion into the world previously dominated by masts and sails.

Funnel

The funnel for the model of the *Sirius* by chance happened to be exactly the diameter of a $\frac{1}{2}$in copper water-pipe. All that was needed was to add the *banding*, which consisted of glued paper strips, the whistle-pipe *brackets* and the *chain-eyes* around the top band. Small eyes were formed in tinned copper wire using round-nosed pliers, leaving a tail about $\frac{1}{8}$in (3mm) long. Holes were drilled after marking

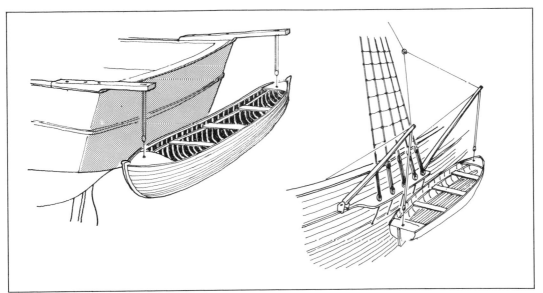

Figure 62 Davits. A fixed stern davit is shown on the left. That on the right consists of two arms hinged to the mizzen chain wale, enabling the boat to be swung clear of the ship's sides when launching.

with a centrepunch, and the eye-tails coated with epoxy resin glue before being pushed into position. The whole funnel was then given three coats of flat white paint from an aerosol can, and the top sector painted matt black. The funnel mounting was made from a block of beech which was painted and glued to the sub-deck, after which the funnel was set in position with epoxy.

The *Great Western* funnel, however, was not so convenient a dimension. It was made up from a sheet of brass wrapped around a wooden core turned to exactly the right diameter. The core extends from the bottom of the funnel to about 1½in (40mm) from the cap, so that the funnel appears to be hollow. The core was coated with epoxy and the brass sheet applied, the whole being then bound tightly with sellotape until the glue had set. The sellotape was then removed, and the seam filed smooth. A funnel cap and foot were

Figure 63 The funnel of Brunel's *Great Western*, showing the whistle pipes and turned cap and foot.

turned from an old brass plumbing fitting and fixed with epoxy resin. Eyes and brackets were added as described previously (*Figure 63*).

Ventilators (*Figure 64*)

The ventilators on the deck of the *Sirius* preceded the brass cowls seen on more modern vessels. They were designed to allow a through-flow of air, and were simply slotted horizontally on each face. They were modelled from pieces of lime suitably shaped, with the slots pressed in with the tip of a sharp modelling knife before painting.

Binnacle

This and other navigational instruments seen on the deck lend themselves well to being turned in brass, and present no particular difficulty. Scale, as always, is the vital consideration.

Paddle wheels (*Figure 65*)

Towards the end of the eighteenth century, paddle steamers first made their appearance, the steam power hesitantly acting as a supplement to the reliable sail. In 1818 the *Savannah* sailed the Atlantic, her paddle wheels turning idly and only occasional attempts being made to apply steam power. It was not until 1838 that the p.s. *Sirius* made the first Atlantic crossing under continuous steam power, followed literally within hours by Brunel's *Great Western*, which was the first steamer designed to provide an Atlantic passenger service. But the paddle steamer as an ocean-going vessel was short-lived, and the rolling gait of this type of ship soon gave way to the more stable screw-driven steamship, of which *Archimedes* was among the first.

Paddle wheels are not as difficult to model as might be expected at first glance. The inner and outer rims and hubs are marked out in ink on masking tape stuck to brass sheet, and carefully fretsawed out using blades designed for metal cutting. The work has to be kept close to the bench support to avoid bending the sheet, and the saw used with steady, even, upright strokes; but otherwise the exercise is no different from the procedure adopted in fretsawing plywood. $\frac{1}{16}$in (1.5mm) wide brass strip for the spokes is not readily available, but this can be cut from brass sheet with a Stanley knife. The best way to do this is to clamp a metal straightedge over the brass sheet onto a cutting surface with two G-clamps, which will hold the straightedge firmly enough not to move when you apply the force needed for the cutting strokes.

The assembly of the wheel must be done over a setting-out drawing if accuracy is to be achieved. Using masking tape to hold the rims and hub in position, apply multi-bond resin to them at the points of intersection of the spokes. Now brush the hardener onto the corresponding intersections on the spokes and set them in position one at a time, following the drawing underneath. When set,

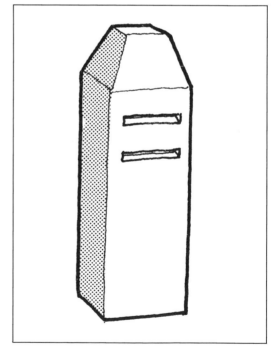

Figure 64 A deck ventilator of a common type encountered on early steamers.

68

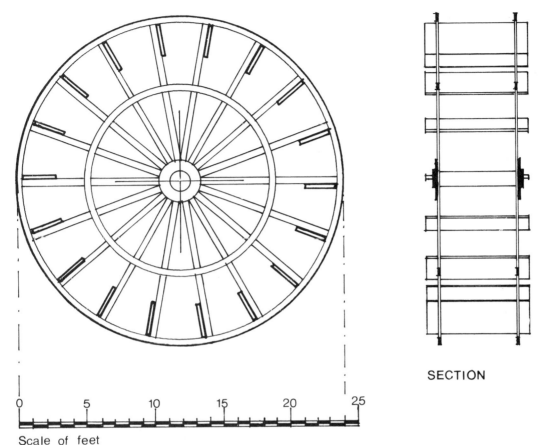

SECTION

Scale of feet

Figure 65 Elevation and section of the paddle wheels of the *Sirius*. The size of the components may be taken from the scale. The mounting of the paddle blades indicates that this is the starboard wheel. The blades on the port wheel would be mounted on the reverse side of the spokes.

remove the wheel frame from the drawing and repeat the procedure for the second frame. When both inner and outer wheel frames are complete, fix a dowel shaft between the hubs with epoxy resin glue. With the assembly on its side, use three wooden blocks of equal size to support the upper frame until the glue has set. The paddles in this case were timber, and were cut from 1mm lime and set in position behind each spoke with epoxy. After painting, drill a hole in the centre of the inner hub and push in a headless pin. Drill a corresponding

hole in the hull, apply epoxy to the hub and secure the wheel. Check carefully that the wheel is supported in perfect alignment while the glue sets.

Paddle wheel housing

The semi-circular inner face of the housing is cut from 3mm thick beech sheet. The 'waste' piece is then screwed down firmly onto the bench over a piece of greaseproof paper. Form the housing from a sheet of brass or alumin-

69

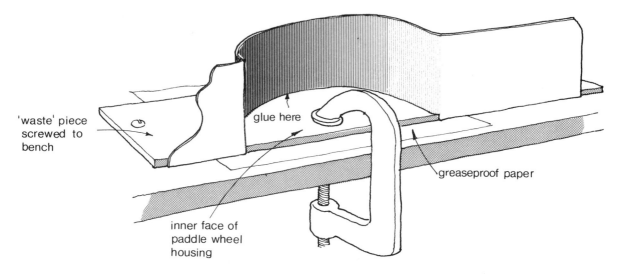

'waste' piece
screwed to
bench

glue here

greaseproof paper

inner face of
paddle wheel
housing

Figure 66 Constructing a paddle wheel housing. The 'waste' piece allows the aluminium sheet to be clamped firmly in position with the inner face of the housing, and the greaseproof paper prevents the assembly from being glued to the bench.

ium, bending it roughly to shape over a thick dowel. Apply epoxy resin glue to the edge of the semi-circular inner piece and sandwich the brass between it and the waste piece, so that the proper shape is held while the glue sets (*Figure* 66). Repeat the procedure for the outer face of the housing, cutting any vents before fixing it to the brass. The whole assembly can now be set in position and painted.

6. The rigging

To the uninitiated eye the rigging of a three-masted sailing vessel appears wildly complicated. Closer examination, however, shows that this complexity arises out of the repetition of a few simple, logical details which can quite easily be followed with a little study. The intention here is to work through the rigging in the same order as it would have been carried out in rigging a real vessel, giving terminology and hints on modelling where necessary. Before making a start, however, some basic definitions will be needed:

Spars   A general term for the timbers which form the masts, yards, gaffs etc., when not referred to by their proper names.

Masts   Vertical fixed spars either built into the body of the hull or fixed to other mast sections. All other spars are able to be moved to meet the requirements of sailing the vessel.

Yards   These are spars attached to the masts, on which square sails are set.

Gaffs and booms   The spars to which the head and foot respectively of fore-and-aft sails are attached.

MASTS

The names of the masts are as follows, from bow to stern:

Two-masted ship: foremast, mainmast.
Three-masted ship: foremast, mainmast, mizzenmast.
Four-masted ship: foremast, mainmast, mizzenmast, aftermast.

The aftermast is known by a variety of terms. For example, in the case of a schooner it is known as the *spanker mast*, with a *jiggermast* and *driver mast* introduced between it and the mizzen if more than four masts were required.

Each mast itself is divided up into sections: lower mast, topmast and topgallant mast (*Figure 68*).

Lower mast

This is the heaviest section, which was only slightly tapered and which passed through the hull with its heel set on the *keelson*. Because of the difficulty of obtaining timber of sufficient girth and length for the masts of larger vessels, the lower mast was often made up of a number of sections and bound together on earlier vessels with rope *wooldings*. These later gave way to iron bands spaced at regular intervals. These *made masts* proved to be considerably stronger than one-piece masts. At the head of the mast the circular section is flattened on either side to take the cheeks which support the trestletrees and crosstrees. Provision is made in these to receive the topmast, which

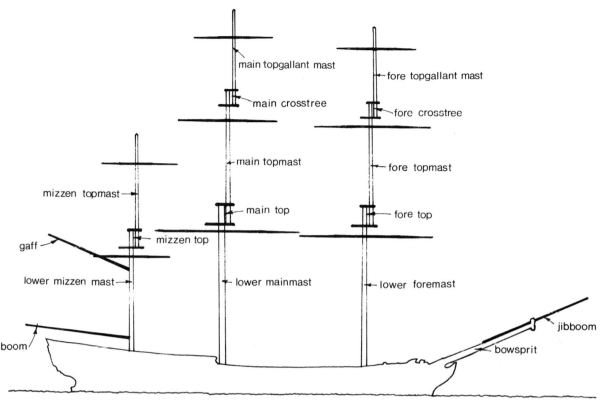

Figure 68 labels: main topgallant mast, main crosstree, main topmast, main top, mizzen topmast, mizzen top, gaff, lower mizzen mast, boom, lower mainmast, fore topgallant mast, fore crosstree, fore topmast, fore top, lower foremast, jibboom, bowsprit

passes through the cap fixed to the head of the mast. A platform is supported on the trestletrees and crosstrees, and the whole construction is known as the top (*Figure 69*). This platform was circular until the end of the seventeenth century, and its purpose was not only to be a sort of landing on the way up the mast, but also to be a vantage point for archers or sharpshooters, when it was known as a *fighting top*. The platform changed through a variety of shapes in the nineteenth century, eventually disappearing altogether and leaving only the trestletrees and crosstrees which were essential to the rigging of the vessel.

Figure 67 The *Cutty Sark*, showing the complexity of the rigging. The most famous of clipper ships, she was launched on the Clyde in 1869, and competed in the race to capture the best of the China tea trade. It seems incredible that this mass of rigging was handled competently by a crew of 28, many of whom were boys.

Figure 68 The names of the mast sections on a typical three-masted vessel.

Topmast

This is generally tapered rather more than the lower mast. It is squared off at the lower end to fit into the housing on the lower mast top, and the structure at the head is known as the *crosstree* (as distinct from the *top* of the lower mast), and consisted of trestletrees, crosstrees and cap, but without a platform (*Figure 70*).

Topgallant mast

This was similar in construction to the topmast but reduced in scale. Sometimes a *topgallant crosstree* was provided into which was fitted the *flagpole* surmounted by a *truck*.

You will find it convenient to construct the

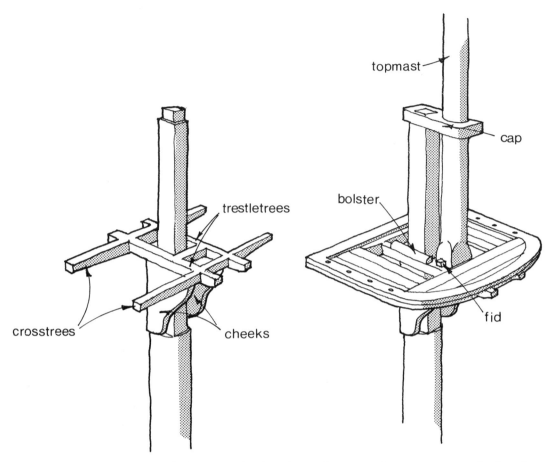

Figure 69 The construction at the lower masthead, known as the top. The platform and topmast are omitted on the diagram on the left for clarity. This form of construction was common in the nineteenth century.

mast-tops first before setting the lower masts in position. Attach the cheeks to the flattened surfaces of the lower mastheads with pva glue, and then fix the trestletrees, which were always parallel to the waterline regardless of any rake in the mast. The crosstrees and blocks are then added as shown, with a bolster on either side to provide a smooth transition for the shrouds which will pass over the top. Finally, add the platform if specified. Note that where the platform was omitted on later nineteenth-century vessels, the length of the crosstrees often varied, becoming shorter on the forward side of the mast and curving away from the bow to achieve a greater angle of bracing to the topmasts (*Figure 71*). It is as well at this stage to construct the topmast so that it can be tried in position to ensure that it will align perfectly with the lower mast when fitted later. The topmast passes through the round hole in the cap, and the squared-off lower end rests in the hole between the block and the forward crosstree. It is prevented from dropping through by a wooden or iron pin (a *fid*).

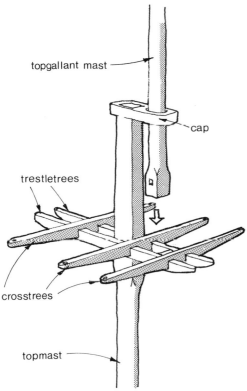

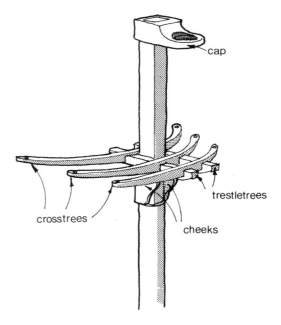

Figure 70 The construction of the topmast head, known as the crosstree.

Figure 71 The top construction on a mid-nineteenth-century ship, showing curved crosstrees to give greater bracing to the topmast.

The lower masts may now be set in position in the hull, commencing with the mizzen and working forward. When this has been done, they must be braced against the loads imposed by the action of the sails and the movement of the vessel. This is effected in the first instance by rigging the *shrouds*. You will need a quantity of rigging cord spun from hemp, which should be available from your local model shop in 20m hanks of various gauge, usually from 0.25mm to 1.6mm. As a guide to selecting your needs, you will find that 0.75mm is a satisfactory size for the shrouds on a ⅛in scale model. For very fine rigging you can use ordinary polyester/cotton button thread in a natural or beige colour. On the subject of colour, you should note that rigging lines fall into two categories:

Standing rigging, which supports the masts and which, once adjusted, was usually treated with tar or pitch as a preservative. These lines should thus be stained black on the model.

Running rigging is the term for the lines which run through blocks and control the setting of the yards and sails. Because of the need to handle them frequently, they remained untreated, and should be represented by natural-coloured cord.

One other point in this connection is that if you are fortunate enough to obtain the actual sizes of the rigging used, note that the figures given represent the circumference rather than the diameter of the ropes. The 18in (460mm) forestay on the *Victory* would therefore be about 6in (150mm) in diameter, which, converted to ⅛in scale, would give a cord diameter of 1/16in (1.6mm).

Before rigging the shrouds it will be necessary to mount the deadeyes on the chain wales.

75

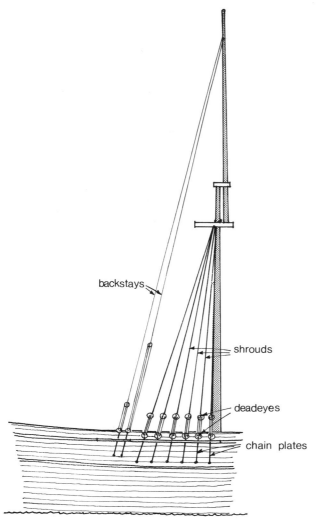

backstays

shrouds

deadeyes

chain plates

Figure 72 The shrouds brace the lower mast and the backstays, the topmast. The tension on all of these rigging lines may be adjusted by means of the deadeyes.

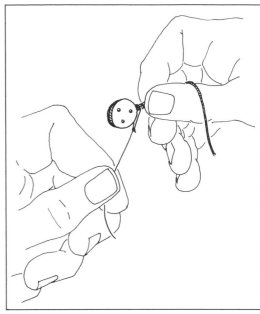

Figure 73 Seizing a deadeye.

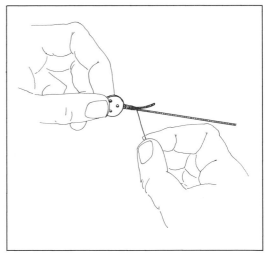

Figure 74 Whipping the shroud to a deadeye.

Mark out the chain bolt positions as follows. Temporarily tie one end of a piece of cord to the mast top and hold it so that it passes through one of the shroud notches in the chain wale and continues *in a straight line* to the level at which the chain bolt is to be fixed. Mark this point, and move the cord to the next shroud notch. As explained previously, each chain plate will be at a different angle, because the shrouds fan out from the mast top (*Figure 72*). Drill the marked points, apply a little epoxy resin glue to the chain bolt, and fix the chain plate and deadeye in position. When one chain wale is complete use pva glue to fix the cover plate in position, and proceed to the next.

Rigging the lower masts

The correct procedure is to commence with the shrouds on the starboard side of the foremast, and to proceed on alternate sides, working sternwards. Cut a length of shroud-cord sufficiently long to reach from the deck to the mast top and back, with a little to spare. A deadeye must now be *seized* to one end of this shroud. Make a slipknot in a 4in (100mm) length of cotton thread, then wind a small length of the shroud around a deadeye allowing about ⅜in (8mm) return. Holding the shroud and its return between finger and thumb close to the deadeye, pass the slipknot over the deadeye and pull firmly (*Figure 73*). Now apply a little pva glue between the shroud and its return, and pinch the two pieces of cord together. The other end of the shroud must now be held firmly (perhaps in your bench vice) so that the cord can be held taut while you pull gently on the deadeye with one hand and use the other to bind, or *whip*, the cotton thread around the two pieces of shroud. Apply tiny quantities of pva glue as you proceed, so that the whipping adheres to the shroud (*Figure 74*).

A lanyard must now be attached between this deadeye and its mate already fixed to the chain wale. Observing the correct location of the holes in the two deadeyes, proceed as

follows. Form a stopknot in the end of an 8in (200mm) length of button thread and apply a little pva glue to the other end, pinching it as it dries to form a hard point; this will make threading a great deal easier. Pass this end through the shroud deadeye from the back, using the lower hole nearest the stern. Pull the lanyard right through until the stopknot engages, and apply pva glue to fix it firmly. The stopknot should be of such a size that it can just be pulled into the hole without being drawn right through. The following sequence should then be adopted.

1 Pass the lanyard through the front of the upper stern-side hole in the lower deadeye.

2 Pass it through the back of the top hole in the upper deadeye.

3 Then through the front of the lower hole in the lower deadeye.

4 Then through the back of the forward-side hole in the top deadeye.

5 Then through the front of the remaining hole in the lower deadeye.

Finally, pull the cord through to form even loops and make a temporary hitch with the end of the lanyard around the shroud just above the deadeye (*Figure 75*). It will not be possible to fix the deadeye accurately as the other end of the shroud is still free.

Take this free end and pass it over the bolster on the starboard side of the foremast, around the mast, back over the same bolster and down on the same side to form the second starboard foremast shroud (*Figure 76*). Carry out the same procedure in fixing a deadeye to the shroud end, ensuring that, when tightened, the distance between the deadeyes corresponds to the requirements of your rigging plan. The distance is usually between three and five deadeye diameters. Attach the lanyard, but do not tighten too much at this stage.

You must now turn your attention to the corresponding pair of shrouds on the port side. Carry out the same procedure here, and continue until all the shrouds have been set on the lower foremast. Where an odd number of

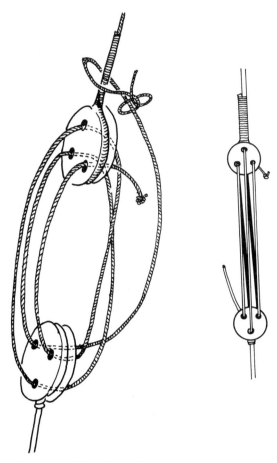

Figure 75 Threading a lanyard through a pair of deadeyes.

shrouds is required on each side of the mast, the last shroud is rigged to the deadeye on the starboard side and taken over the mast top and down to the deadeye on the port side, instead of returning on the same side. Now proceed with the mainmast shrouding, continuing until all the lower masts have their shrouds in position but still not finally tightened. Do not cut off the spare lengths of lanyard until final tightening has been carried out at a later stage.

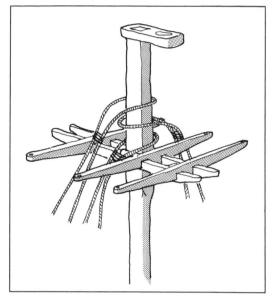

Figure 76 The method of fixing the shrouds to the masthead.

Rigging the bowsprit (*Figure 77*)

Usually a *jibboom* was set on top of the bowsprit to carry stays from the upper masts. The bowsprit itself was fastened to the stem by means of *gammoning*, and a *cap* was provided at the tip through which passed the jibboom. The heel of the jibboom usually sat in a shaped saddle and was lashed in position. In later vessels a hinged iron saddle was used which enabled the jibboom to be withdrawn when in port to avoid damage and to reduce the overall length of the vessel. The bowsprit was braced by means of a shroud on either side and a heavy *bobstay*, usually a chain, fixed back to the stem below. Towards the end of the nineteenth century the bobstay was often a solid iron bar. A *martingale* or *dolphin-striker* was fixed below the cap, and was used to brace the jibboom.

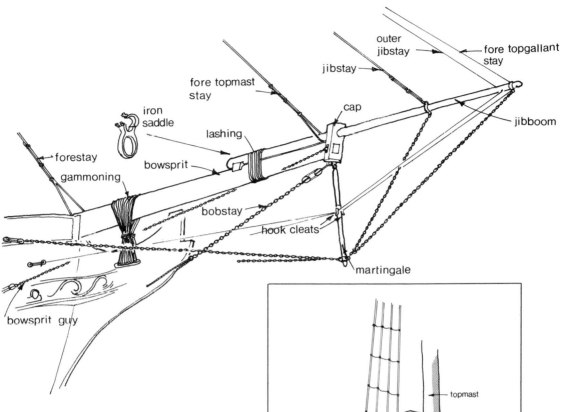

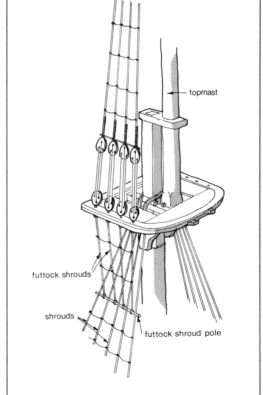

Figure 77 This bowsprit has a jibboom set on it which has been fixed through a cap and lashed in front of the saddle. The conventional method of rigging is shown. Note where chain is used in preference to rope.

Rigging the upper masts (*Figure 78*)

Smaller diameter deadeyes will be required at this level. Loop a piece of wire around a deadeye and give it a twist or two to hold it in position, then snip off the excess wire. Apply solder to the twist. Pass the other end of the wire downwards through the edge of the platform or through a small hole in the ends of

Figure 78 The lower mast top, showing the mounting of the upper and lower shrouds.

the crosstree. Using a pair of round-nosed pliers, form a small eyelet immediately below the top, once again snipping off the excess and applying a small amount of solder. Once all the deadeyes are in position, use a very fine brush to paint the wire matt black. Now cut a piece of wire to the correct length of the *futtock shroud pole*, and bind this in position by means of slipknots around the two outer shrouds, after which a dot of epoxy resin may be applied to each point where the pole crosses the shrouds. It is important to fix the pole firmly, as it takes a fair amount of strain. The futtock shrouds themselves may now be attached, tied to the pole between each shroud and running up to the corresponding eyelet.

The purpose of the futtock shrouds, apart from bracing the upper mast shrouds, was to allow the crew quick access to the top, and for this reason they carried the continuation of the *ratlines* which were tied ladder-fashion across the shrouds below. It must have called for considerable courage to climb this overhanging route in calm weather, let alone during a storm at sea. The only alternative was to squeeze through the narrow opening in the platform which permits the passage of the shrouds over the bolsters; and for this reason the opening was known as the *lubber's hole*.

The topmast shrouds are installed using the same procedure as described for the lower mast shrouds, and in the same sequence. The shrouds to the topgallant mast follow. You will note, no doubt with some relief, that the lower deadeyes are fixed directly to the topgallant crosstrees without the need for futtock shrouds.

Rigging stays and backstays

The stays are now rigged as shown in Figure 79, commencing with the mainstays. The forestays and the mizzen stay are next, and the rigging continues upwards in the same order. Take careful note of the considerable variation in the diameter of the stays required by the rigging plan. The general principle used for fastening the stays to the masts was to form a

loop which passed over a cleat fixed into the back of the mast. The forend of the stay was usually whipped to a heart-shaped block, with a lanyard fixing to allow adjustment. The object of the backstays was to brace the topmast and topgallant mast, and there were usually two backstays on each side of the ship for each mast section. They were fixed to eyes in iron bands around the mast at the upper end and usually to deadeyes at the lower end.

Trimming the rigging

With the standing rigging complete, you can now make final adjustments to remove any sag from the lines and to bring the whole to just the right degree of tension without introducing unnecessary strain. Only moderate tightening of a lanyard will induce a surprising amount of tension into its shrouds, so it is necessary to check after each adjustment that the masts are correctly aligned both from ahead and from the side; and once you are completely satisfied, apply a drop of pva glue to each knot, snipping off the excess thread when the glue has dried.

Ratlines

Before tying the ratlines, a *sheer pole* must be fitted immediately above the upper row of deadeyes. This device prevented the shrouds from drawing together under the weight of the men climbing the ratlines. A piece of wire 1mm in diameter is cut to the correct length and painted matt black. It is then inserted into the noose of a slipknot tied around one of the end shrouds. The slipknot is pulled tight; and after carrying out the same procedure on the shroud at the other end, the sheer pole will be held firmly while you tie the pole to the intermediate shrouds. A tiny spot of epoxy touched to each intersection will hold the sheer pole permanently in position.

In comparison with the 0.75mm cord used for the shrouds, a fine cotton thread will be needed to give an adequate representation of the ratlines. The knots used to tie the ratlines

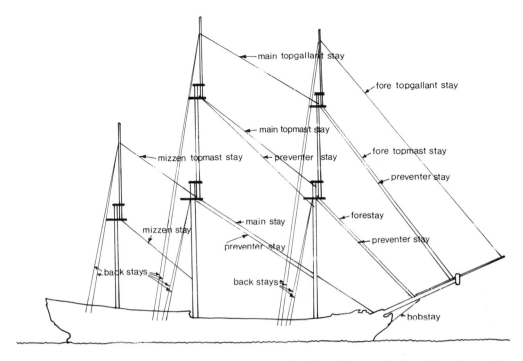

Figure 79 The names and location of the stays on a typical three-masted vessel.

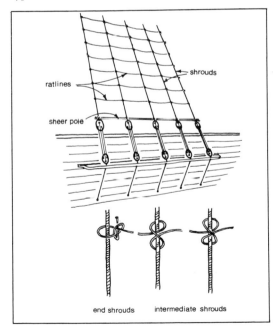

Figure 80 The method of fixing the sheerpole and fastening the ratlines to the shrouds.

to the shrouds were designed firstly to tighten under load, so that they would not slip down the shrouds, and secondly to allow water to drain away easily. Small as they will be, these same knots should be used on the model for authenticity, and the illustration shows how they should be tied. As you work your way up the shrouds spacing the ratlines about 15in (380mm) apart, you will find it increasingly difficult to get your finger and thumb into the narrowing spaces, and it is recommended that you use two pairs of pointed tweezers to help make this rather tedious exercise somewhat faster and easier. Leave a small amount of spare thread at either end of each ratline, and when you have completed perhaps a dozen, apply a dot of pva glue to each intersection. Only when a complete set of shrouds has had its ratlines tied should you snip off the unwanted ends (*Figure 80*).

During the latter half of the nineteenth century, deadeyes and lanyards gave way to *turnbuckles* as a means of altering the tension of the shrouds, and these were often fixed inboard rather than over the rail. At the same time wire standing rigging became commonplace, and chain was often used for much of the heavier running rigging. Your rigging plan and the period of the ship you are modelling will guide you in the selection of materials.

YARDS

It had been appreciated at an early stage in the development of the square sail that the stress which the sail imposed on the yard decreased towards the outer ends of the yard. This made it possible to reduce weight by tapering the yards. Until the mid-nineteenth century the centre portion of the yard was usually eight-sided before the taper commenced, but later this became circular in section.

Shaping spars

The most convenient method of making precisely tapered spars in accordance with the rigging plan is to turn them on a lathe, but satisfactory results can also be achieved by starting with a dowel which holds the largest diameter required and using a surform to make a square taper first (*Figure 81A*). The corners of the square portion are then carefully shaved off. It is not difficult to assess by eye that the eight sides so produced are evenly tapered (B). Finally, the taper is rounded off with glasspaper (C).

The lower yards

These were never lowered during sailing, and were attached to iron swivels called *trusses*. The weight of these yards was supported by chain *slings* which passed through the lubber's hole and over a cleat fixed to the after side of the mast (*Figure 82*). Before the nineteenth century the truss was often simply a thick rope looped twice around the mast. The weight of

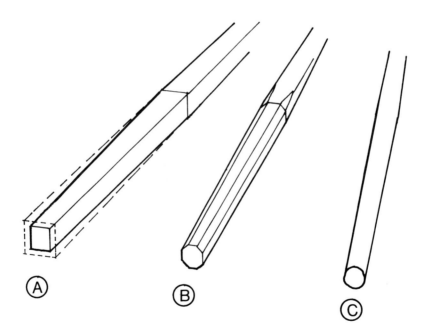

Figure 81 Shaping spars without using a lathe.

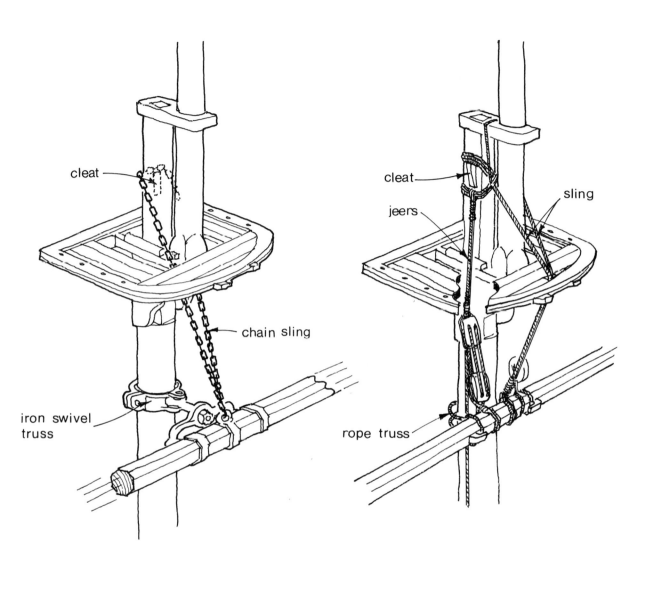

cleat

chain sling

iron swivel
truss

1860

cleat

jeers

sling

rope truss

1800

Figure 82 The means of slinging the lower yard from the mast top, showing the development over a 60-year period

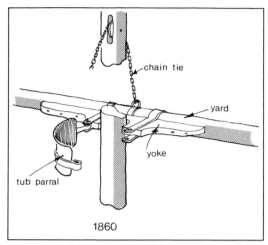

Figure 83 The attachment of the upper yard to the topmast, showing the tub parral and yoke.

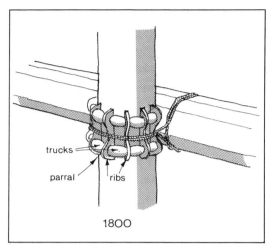

Figure 84 An earlier method of attaching the upper yard to the topmast, using a wooden parral.

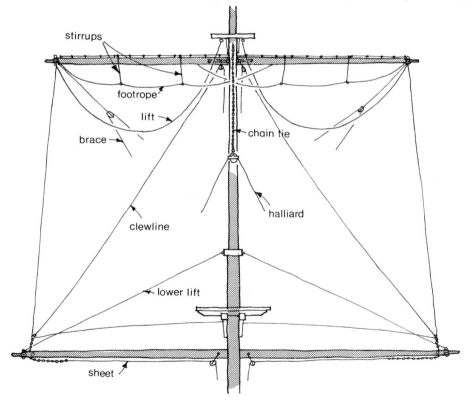

Figure 85 Aft view of a set topsail. The footropes can be seen, by which means the crew were able to climb out to the yard ends when furling or reefing the sail.

the yard was taken on a system of heavy blocks
and tackle called *jeers*. If it became necessary to
repair or replace the lower yards as a result of
damage sustained in battle, the jeers were used
to hoist the yard down to deck level.

The upper yards

From the mid-nineteenth century these were
attached to the mast by means of a loose-
fitting broad iron band known as a *tub parral*
which was split and hanged to allow removal
from the mast (*Figure 83*). The parral was held
firmly to the yard by means of a wooden yoke,
and the whole yard assembly could be raised
and lowered on the mast by means of a *tie
chain* which passed through an opening in the
mast over a sheave. The tie chain was attached
to a *halliard block* which had rope tackle
leading to deck level. On earlier vessels the
parral consisted of a number of barrel-shaped
wooden rollers separated by ribs. The supporting rope was threaded through the rollers
before being looped and tied around the yards
(*Figure 84*). Movement of the yard was
effected by either a single or a pair of rope ties
which were in turn attached to halliard blocks.

The object of raising and lowering the
upper yards was to expedite the furling and
reefing of the sails. The yard would be lowered
in order to give access from the top or topmast
head, and the men would then climb out
towards the yard ends using the *footropes* slung
on *stirrups* beneath the yard, and pull up the
sail by hand over the forward side of the yard.
Reef points – two or three horizontal rows of
short pieces of line attached to the fore and aft
sides of the sail – would be used to tie around
the sail to hold it to the yard. The sail could
thus be furled completely or reduced in area to
suit sailing conditions (*Figure 85*).

Until the mid-nineteenth century, before
the introduction of reefing, the sails on the
lower yards were divided into two unequal
parts. The lower part, known as a *bonnet*, was
laced to the foot of the sail above in an
ingenious manner which allowed it to be
removed swiftly when it became necessary to
shorten the sail (*Figure 86*).

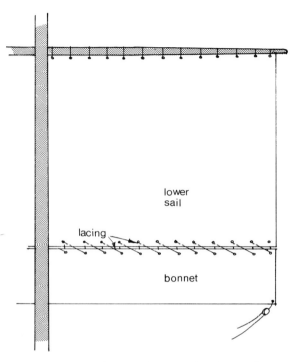

Figure 86 Before the introduction of reefing, sail
area was reduced when necessary by removing the
bonnet which was laced to the foot of the mainsail.

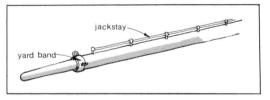

Figure 87 The jackstay, fitted atop the yard, to
which the sail was bent.

Up until the beginning of the nineteenth
century, sails were generally attached to the
yards by a simple system of lacing, which
passed over the yard and through eyelets in
the head of the sail. This gave way to the
jackstay, which was a rope fixed through a
series of eyebolts screwed into the top of the
yard providing a fixing for the sail. In due
course the rope was superseded by a solid iron
rod (*Figure 87*).

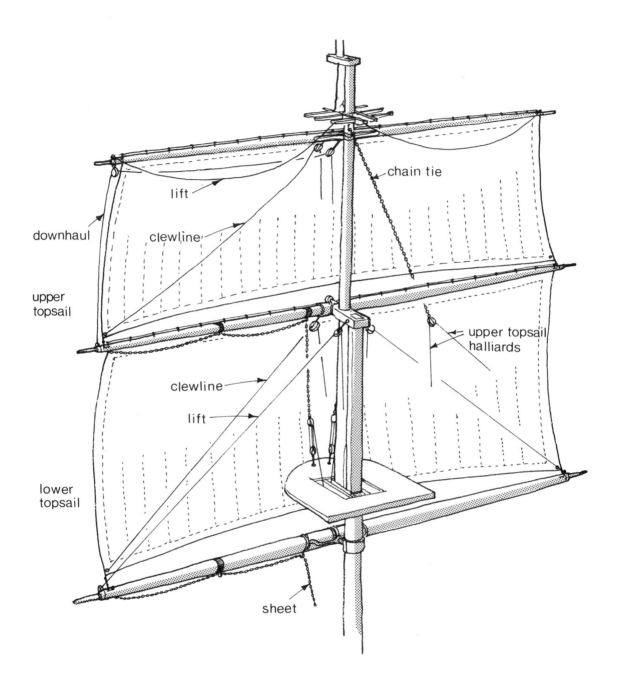

downhaul

lift

clewline

chain tie

upper
topsail

clewline

lift

upper topsail
halliards

lower
topsail

sheet

Figure 88 The double topsail, introduced in the mid-nineteenth century. The additional lower yard is attached to the lower mast cap by means of a swivel truss.

The jackstay may be modelled by first using a centrepunch to mark off the eyelet locations on the yard held in a vice. These may then be drilled, taking care not to drill right through the spar. Small lengths of tinned wire of slightly larger diameter than the holes are then forced in and trimmed off with wire cutters. You will find that the small inset of the cutting edges of this tool will leave about the right amount of wire projecting if the cut is made while holding the cutters close up against the yard. A tiny amount of solder is now applied to the tip of each piece of wire, and one end of the jackstay soldered in position. Solder the other end, then work from the middle outwards to prevent the heat of the iron desoldering the joints already made.

Double topsail (Figure 88)

With the growth of sail area as an answer to the constant demand for greater speed, topsails began to reach unmanageable proportions. In the mid-nineteenth century the double topsail made its appearance, dividing the old topsail into two parts, each with its own yard. The upper yard retained the fixing to the topmast used previously, while the new lower yard was attached with a swivel truss to the lower mast cap. A second set of tackle for the adjustment of the lower yard was provided.

Lifts

The primary function of the lift is to support the ends of the yards to prevent them from

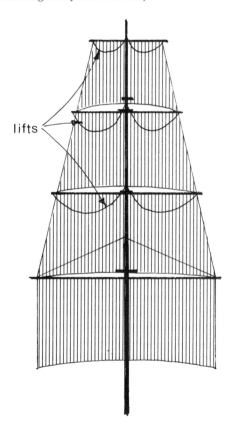

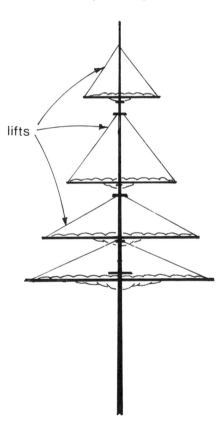

Figure 89A The upper yard lifts hang in loops behind the sail when the sails are set.

Figure 89B The upper yard lifts support the yard tips when the sails are furled.

sagging under the weight of the sail they carried. In earlier vessels the lifts passed from an eye in an iron band on the yardtip over a system of blocks and tackle and down the mast, eventually being belayed to the fife rail at deck level. The lifts could also be used to trim the yard out of the horizontal, and to work in conjunction with the halliards in raising and lowering the yard. However, after the introduction of the double topsail, the lifts for the upper yards were simplified to become a single supporting rope or wire from each yard tip to a fixed point on the mast. This meant that when the yards were raised the lifts were inoperative and hung in loops below the yard (*Figure 89*). The lower topsail yard was not provided with lifts, but instead had its tips supported by means of downhauls attached to the upper yards.

Braces
These were ropes leading from the ends of the yards (frequently attached to the same band as the lifts) by which the yards could be trimmed to the wind. Braces to mizzen yards always led forward, while all others led aft, passing either directly to deck level or via blocks attached to stays or shrouds.

Studding sails (Figure 90)
These were used to increase the sail area in order to give greater speed when running free, with the wind on either quarter. The studding sail *boom* lay directly over the yard and ran through two iron bands, one fixed at the tip of the yard and the other a little way in. When required the boom could be extended and lashed, and the tack of the studding sail attached to its tip.

Spritsail yard (Figure 91)
From the seventeenth century onwards, a square spritsail was rigged on a yard below the bowsprit, and a *spritsail topmast*, complete with platform, yard and sail, was to be found at the end of the bowsprit of larger vessels. The spritsail topsail was impractical, obstructing the view forward and subject to damage in

port, yet it was retained for more than a century. When it was eventually replaced by the *jibsail*, the spritsail below the bowsprit was still retained for some time. Despite the hazards involved in its use, it appeared on vessels well into the nineteenth century.

Making yard bands
There are a number of ways of making these, perhaps the simplest being to glue one side of a narrow black paper strip and wind it around the yard two or three times. This can then be drilled through into the yard to take the eyes, which are formed in wire of a suitable gauge and set in the holes with epoxy resin glue. Alternatively, the bands can be cut from brass or aluminium tube before fitting them on the yard and drilling as before. You might also consider turning them on a lathe if the right diameter metal tube is not available. All yard bands and eyes should be fitted before you attempt to attach the yard to the mast. Remember that iron bands were not generally in use until the beginning of the nineteenth century, before which time rope ends were lashed to the yards.

GAFFS AND BOOMS

In the mid-eighteenth century the lateen sail, which had been in general use as a mizzen sail for nearly 300 years, was gradually superseded by the *gaff sail*, which overcame many of the limitations of the lateen sail. The gaff sail was bent to a *gaff* at the head and a *boom* at the foot, each of which were in turn attached to the mizzen mast by means of jaws and a parral. In its lowered position the boom rested on a *saddle*, a semi-circular wooden moulding fixed to the mast. The boom was adjusted from above by a *topping lift*, and was set by means of a pair of *sheets*. The gaff had *peak halliards* above and vangs on either side for setting (*Figure 92*). On larger vessels a *spencer mast* was fitted immediately abaft the mizzen mast to carry the boom and gaff jaws as well as the *sail hoops* which held the sail to the mast (*Figure 93*).

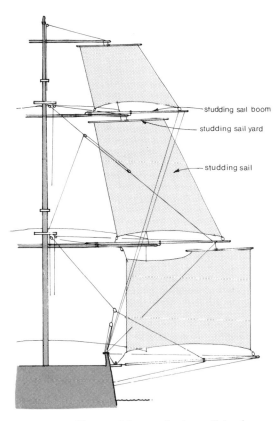

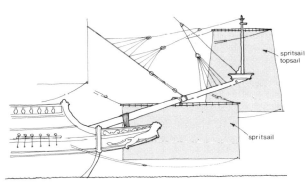

Figure 91 The spritsail topmast found on many seventeenth-century ships. The spritsail was retained for some time after the spritsail topmast had been discarded.

Figure 90 The studding sails (stuns'ls), shown shaded, added considerably to the sail area when extended. Each sail had its own yard attached to the tip of the yard above, and its outermost lower corner was fixed to the studding boom lashed to the yard below.

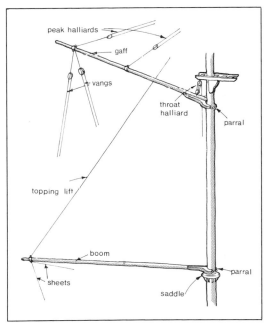

Figure 92 Mizzen mast with gaff, boom and conventional rigging.

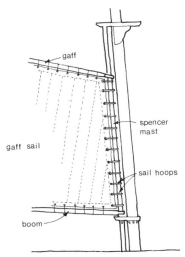

Figure 93 A spencer mast fixed behind the mizzen mast carries the gaff sail and its spars.

DEADEYES AND BLOCKS

Deadeyes

As has already been stated, reasonably satisfactory hardwood deadeyes are usually available at model shops, and come in three sizes: 3mm, 5mm and 7mm. These correspond with ⅛in scale representations of 12in, 18in and 24in diameter. If these sizes do not meet your needs, then a hardwood dowel could be turned on a lathe, grooved, and then cut to the correct widths. Finally, drill the three holes using a miniature drill press, before glasspapering to a smooth finish. In making your own deadeyes you will have the opportunity to overcome the one weakness of ready-made ones: the holes through these seem rarely to be accurately spaced.

Blocks

Single, double and triple hardwood blocks are also available in a range of sizes, but the method described here will produce an acceptable block to exactly the size required. Cut a 3 or 4in length (75–100mm) of, say, 3mm × 2mm mahogany strip, and plane or glasspaper it down to the correct cross-sectional area. Mark off the required lengths of the blocks in pencil, and use a centrepunch to indent the locations of holes required through the blocks. A miniature drill press will ensure that these holes are vertical and parallel to one another. Reclamp the strip in a vice between two pieces of waste wood and saw through on the pencil lines in order to separate the blocks. Now, using a pair of needle-nosed tweezers to handle the tiny block, clamp the drilled sides in the vice and make a shallow sawcut with a fine-bladed saw lengthwise on each of the undrilled faces. Finally, remove the block, hold it in a pair of flat-nosed tweezers, and rub it on glasspaper in order to round off the corners (*Figure 94*). To mount the block, make a slipknot in a length of thread, pass it round the grooved side of the block and pull it tight, after which the thread can be secured with a spot of pva glue on the knot (*Figure 95*).

SAILS

The model you have rigged up to this point is complete except for the sails and associated rigging. Many display models are left without sails for a variety of reasons. It might be felt that their inclusion would conceal much of the detailed work on other rigging. Perhaps the proliferation of cords and threads would make it more difficult to understand the purpose of the standing and yard rigging. The type of model you are constructing will to some extent determine whether or not sails should be included, but even the realism of a waterline or scenic model would not be impaired by bare yards, for vessels were often seen in port in this state.

If the decision is made to show the sails, then you must consider in what manner they are to be depicted: all furled, fully set, or in some of the thousand variations which lie between these two, covering the possibilities of partially set or reefed sails.

Square sails

Square sails were rarely if ever square in shape, their name probably deriving from the fact that they were set initially square to the fore-and-aft line of the vessel. The sails on lower yards, and spritsails, were generally rectangular in shape, but the upper sails were trapezoidal, the angle of their sides relating to the changing lengths of successive yards.

You will need some very finely-woven fabric in order to achieve scale realism, such as poplin or lawn. Sailcloth is rarely pure white, and if the right off-white shade is not available, your cloth can be dyed in a weak tea solution. Tape a piece of this fabric onto a flat surface and mark off the various seams lightly in pencil. Working carefully to scale, start with the *tabling*, which is a 12in (300mm) border all round (in practice, a double thickness of sailcloth), then divide the balance up into 24in (600mm) vertical strips, leaving equal odd strips at the two sides if necessary. Now mark on the horizontal *reef bands* as required.

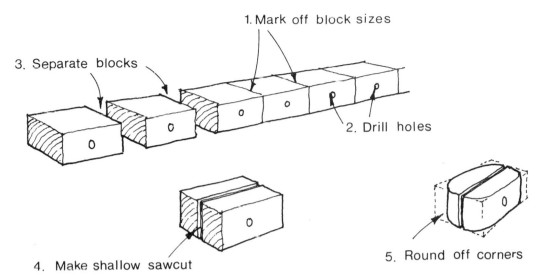

1. Mark off block sizes

3. Separate blocks

2. Drill holes

4. Make shallow sawcut

5. Round off corners

Figure 94 A simple method of making rigging blocks.

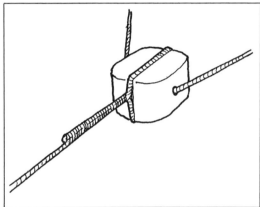

Figure 95 Seizing a block to its rigging line.

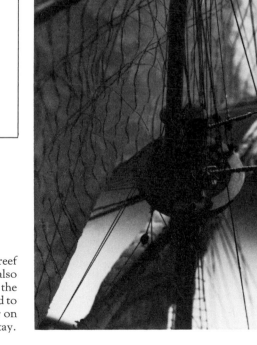

Figure 96 Topsail of the *San Felipe*. Notice the reef points fixed to the reef bands. Crowsfeet can also be seen attached to the forward part of the platform. These extended down to a block seized to the forestay, and were intended to reduce wear on the foot of the topsail as it flapped against the stay.

Remove the sail from the drawing surface and, setting your sewing machine to its smallest stitch, use a fine, natural or beige-coloured cotton to sew along each pencil line to represent the seams. A piece of 0.25mm rigging cord is now stitched by hand using very fine cotton all the way round the edge of the sail to represent the *leech ropes* at the sides and *head* and *foot ropes* at the top and bottom respectively. At the lower two corners of the sail is a *clew*, which on larger vessels was a triple-eyed metal fitting; but a simple loop in the leech line is probably sufficient for your requirements. Finally, stitch onto the reef bands on both sides of the sail short pieces of thread representing the 24in (600mm) long *reef points*, by which the sails were attached to the yards when reefing (*Figure 97*). A reef point occurs in line with each vertical seam in the sail cloth, and is attached by means of a *reef cringle*, which you can represent simply by the knot fastening it to the reef band.

The sail may now be bent to the yard, either by lacing so that it hangs below the yard if no jackstay is available, or with *robands* 24in (600mm) apart tied directly to the jackstay, with the sail on the forward side of the yard. Attach lines to the clews of lower sails to represent the *sheets* which run aft, and the *tacks* which run forward. The sheets of upper sails are taken through a hole in the yard-end immediately below, across the yard towards the mast, through a block and down to deck level. A third short line is first lashed to a block before attaching it to the clew, and this is the *clewgarnet* (or *clewline* on upper sails). This runs up the aft side of the sail to a block fixed to the yard a little way in from the yard end, through another block fixed to the yard yoke, and then down the mast to deck level. This was used to clew the corners of the sail up to the yard.

On the forward side of the sail are the *buntlines*, usually only a pair on upper sails but several on the lower. These are hitched to the sail foot ropes and run vertically through *bullseyes* fixed to the reef bands (centrally between the sail seams so as to avoid conflict with the reef points), through blocks attached to the jackstay. From there they are run across to a set of blocks fixed to the underside of the top, and then down the mast on the aft side of the sail to deck level, where they are belayed to the fife rail (*Figure 97*).

These four control lines are repeated on each square sail on each mast. If your model has double topsails, then you will need, in addition, a downhaul on each end of the yard, fixed to the yard tip, run down to a block at the end of the yard below, up again through another block, horizontally along the yard to a block fixed to the yoke, then down the mast to deck level.

Fore-and-aft-sails

The gaff sail and spanker are distinct in their shape as well as some of the terminology. The sail border nearest the mast is known as the *luff*, with a luff rope stitched to it. The eye or loop at the top of this is the *throat cringle*, while that at the foot is the *tack cringle*. The leech line furthest from the mast has a *peak cringle* at the head and a *clew cringle* at the foot; and the seams in the sail run parallel to the leech line. The head and foot of the sail are attached to the gaff and boom by means of lacing or separate *seizings*, and the luff to the mast by loose spiral lacings or metal hoops. These allow the whole sail and gaff to be collapsed onto the boom for furling (*Figure 98*). There were no separate control lines for this sail, as those for the gaff and boom met this need (*Figure 99*).

Staysails

As their name implies, these usually triangular sails were set on the stays which supported the masts. Each was described by the name of the mast to which the highest point of the stay was attached: main topmast staysail, foremast topgallant staysail and so on. As in the case of the gaff sail, that part of the sail attached to the stay was known as the *luff*, the other two sides being the *leech* and the *foot*. Once again, the sail

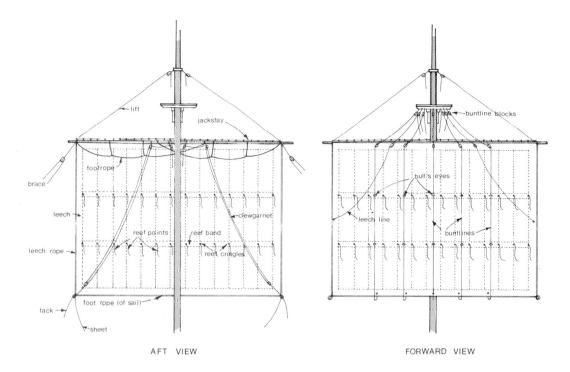

AFT VIEW　　　　　　　　　　　　　FORWARD VIEW

Figure 97 Aft and forward views of a mainsail showing the rigging, and names of the principal sail components.

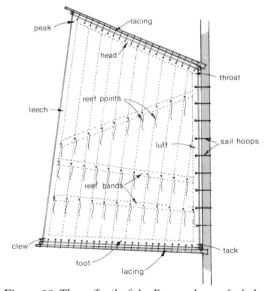

Figure 98 The gaff sail of the *Bounty* shown furled on the boom. Captain Bligh may be seen pacing the quarterdeck below.

Figure 99 The component parts of the gaffsail.

93

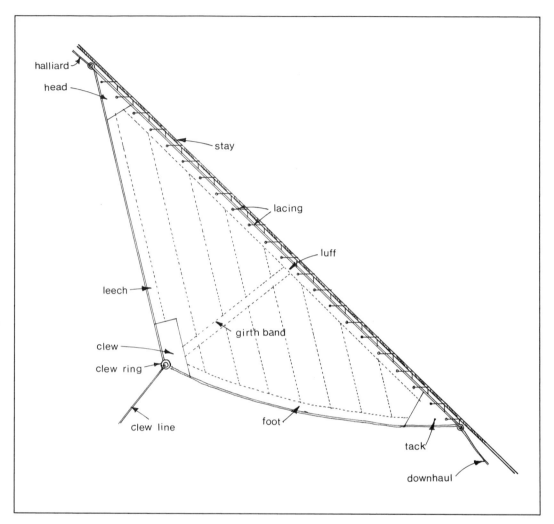

Figure 100 The component parts of the staysail.
The jibsail is very similar in construction.

seams ran parallel to the leech, and *head, tack*
and *clew cringles* were as described for for-and-
aft sails. Attachment to the stay was effected
by means of simple lacing, or, in the case of
wire stays, iron staysail loops were used.
Control of the staysails was effected by means
of sheets fixed to the clew ring and then taken
down to rail level, and halliards and

downhauls enabled them to be run up or
down the stays (*Figure 100*).

Jibsails are in the same classification as
staysails, being attached to the stays which run
forward to the jibboom. These have the same
control system as that described for the
staysails.

7. Displaying the model

Long hours of painstaking work have finally brought their reward, and you are now the proud possessor of a model ship which almost certainly has turned out considerably better than your self-critical forecast had anticipated. And the end result is by no means only the model, for you will have gained a wealth of knowledge of the shipwright's trade and the terminology of sailing vessels. You will be able to indicate with confidence the futtock shrouds, the sail clewed up in the bunt, and explain the difference between lanyards and ratlines. Even more important, you will have learned by your mistakes, and will have decided that next time you will use a different technique for the construction of that particular part which you consider less than perfect.

The materials you have used are durable, and the model will last a long time, at least until it has been admired by your children's grandchildren. Therefore, consideration must be given to how it is to be protected, displayed and lit. A glass case is essential, not only because it will protect the model from the destructive effects of dust, but because it will also prevent unskilled fingers from making adjustments to the rigging or deck fittings. For this reason, when the model is finally enclosed you must make it really difficult to reopen the case, so that it will not be an exercise undertaken casually. On the other hand, sealing it permanently is not advised – imagine the frustration of knocking a yard a few degrees out of true while lifting the display case into position, knowing that you could never make the required adjustment!

Glass display cases may be bought ready-made, but they are expensive and the range available will not suit all models. A simple and inexpensive method of making your own case is described below.

Dimensions

Determine the internal dimensions required, bearing in mind firstly any limitations of the display location, and secondly the type of model you have constructed. You may need rather more base area for the display if the sea or other scenic items are to be included. There is no need to make the height of the case greater than about 2in (50mm) more than the highest point of the model, nor need the width be much more than the length of the longest yard.

Glass

For a case up to 39in × 24in (1m × 600m), 24oz (3mm) glass may be used, and the method described here is satisfactory. For larger panels it will be necessary to use thicker glass and a more conventional means of framing, making use of metal sections to give greater strength.

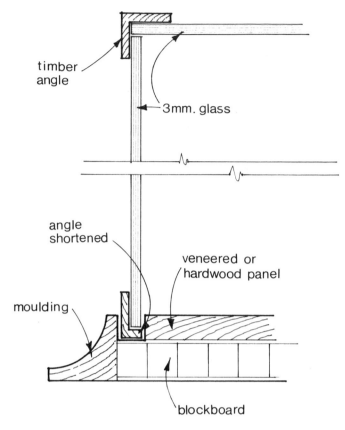

timber angle

3mm. glass

angle shortened

veneered or hardwood panel

moulding

blockboard

Figure 101 Section through a glass case.

The glass must be cut with some accuracy, and if you are ordering it, draw the attention of the supplier to this requirement. Having determined the desired internal dimensions, calculate the glass sheet sizes as follows:

Sides: Internal height + depth of glazing rebate × internal length + 6mm
Ends: Internal height + depth of glazing rebate × internal width
Top: Depth + 6mm × width + 6mm

You will also need a tube of colourless silicone rubber sealant – Aquaria, manufactured by Dow Corning (UK agents Hansil Ltd., Byfleet, Surrey) being recommended.

Baseboard

If you intend to use a piece of solid timber with an attractive grain for your baseboard, it will need to be well-matured and reasonably thick so that it will not warp in time. It is probably safer to use a sheet of 1in (25mm) blockboard to which a second sheet of similar thickness is screwed and glued, with its upper surface suitably veneered. This method has the advantage of allowing the easy formation of a rebate to receive the glass, as the detail shows (*Figure 101*). It is convenient at this point to apply felt pads or thin rubber feet to the underside of the baseboard, if required. The baseboard must be constructed first as it forms a template for the glasswork, and in this connection a small piece of masking tape should be stuck to each corner of the baseboard to provide a tolerance between it and the glass.

Glazing

An extra pair of hands makes this exercise a good deal easier and less alarming, and you will need a firm table on which to work, which can be left undisturbed for a few days. First clean the glass thoroughly with methylated spirits. Then, using small G-clamps, fix a small block of wood to the two top corners of each of the side panels, precisely ⅛in (3mm) in from the vertical edges. Cut the nozzle of the silicone sealant tube and squeeze out a strip ⅛in (3mm) wide onto the edge of one of the end panels (*Figure 102*). Hold one of the side panels in position on the baseboard, and bring the end panel to meet it so that the sealant makes contact. Take great care that the sealant touches no other part of the glass, as it is extremely difficult to remove, both before and after setting. The two sheets should automatically be correctly positioned, the top by the wooden block and the bottom by the baseboard. Now apply three or four pieces of masking tape around the outside corner to hold the sheets together, and ensure that they are at right angles (*Figure 103*). Immediately repeat the procedure with the other end panel,

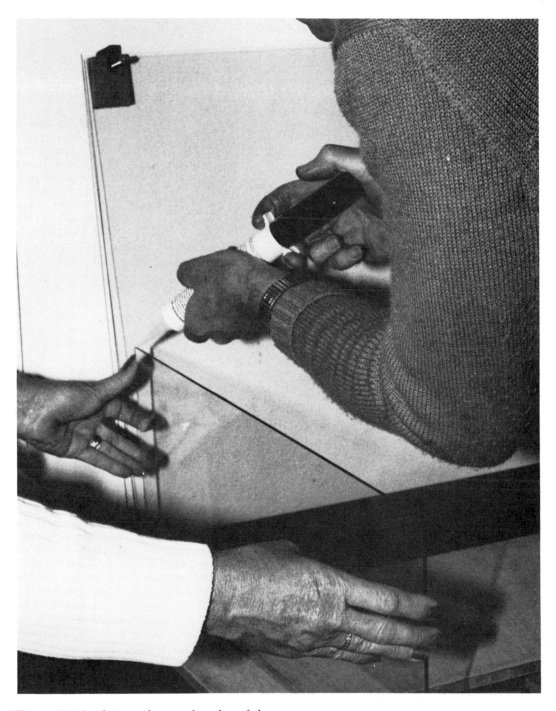

Figure 102 Applying sealant to the edge of the glass.

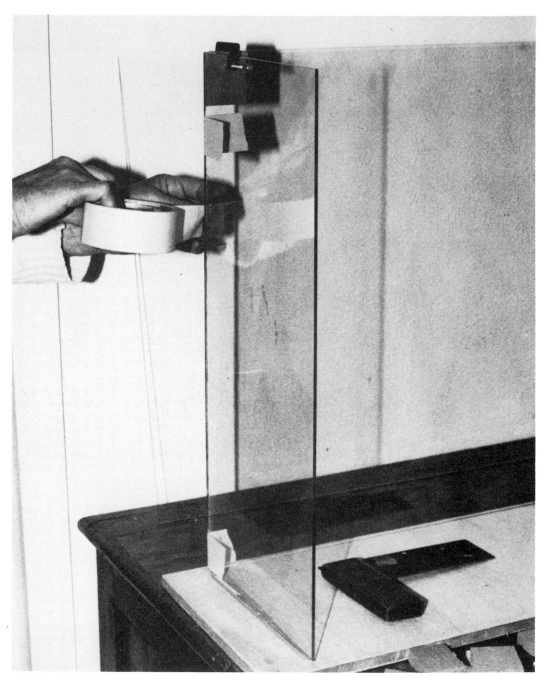

Figure 103 Taping the first two sheets of glass together. Note the block and G-clamp positioning the top corner of the case.

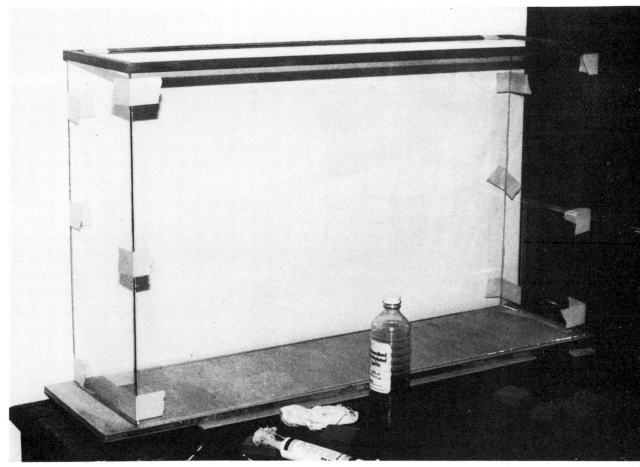

Figure 104 The four sides and the top of the case have been joined, and the mitred wooden angle frame is shown fitted around the top.

and, when that has been secured, apply sealant to the remaining two vertical edges and fix the second side panel in position. Finally, remove the wooden blocks, squeeze out the sealant onto the top edges and set the top panel carefully into position. It is important that the whole of the glass-jointing operation is carried out without a break (either to the glass or the time-schedule!) as the initial set of the sealant would be affected if any appreciable time-lapse were to occur. The sealant cures in about 48 hours, and it is possible to lift the glass after

about 12 hours; but on no account attempt to move or touch it before this.

Framing

For this you will need some timber angle, available usually from timber merchants, in a small range of sizes in obeche or other woods. You will find that a $\frac{5}{8}$in $\times \frac{5}{8}$in $\times \frac{1}{8}$in ($15 \times 15 \times 3$mm) angle gives an attractive, slender appearance, and to enhance this further a wood dye may be applied to the angle before

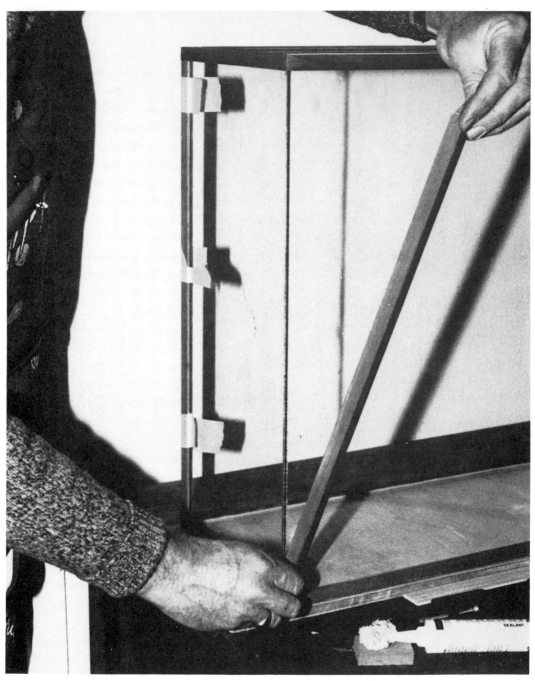

Figure 105 One of the wooden angle uprights is fitted in position.

Figure 106 A wooden moulding is pinned and glued to the baseboard, forming a rebate to receive the glasswork.

constructing the frame. Suitable dyes are Colron Wood Dye, manufactured by Sterling Roncraft, Sheffield, England, and Furniglas Long Life Wood Colour, made by Evode Ltd, Stafford, England. Both these dyes are available in several wood effects, such as American walnut, teak or oak.

Start by cutting four pieces of angle with mitred corners to form the top of the case. Apply a thin strip of silicone sealant to the inside of each leg of one of the angles, and press it carefully into position on the top of the glass. Proceed in turn with each of the angles, using a small quantity of pva glue to join the mitres (*Figure 104*). Leave the case to dry for 12 hours, then lift it from the baseboard and up-end it so that the frame for the base of the glass can be attached. Before fixing these four mitred pieces, however, it is necessary to cut one leg of each angle short so that it does not project beyond the inner face of the glass (*Figure 101*). Fix the framing as described previously, and leave to set. Finally, cut the four uprights with perfectly square ends to fit exactly between the upper and lower frames (*Figure 105*). Once the sealant has cured you will find that the whole case, heavy as it is, can be lifted by hooking your fingers under the edges of the top frame, which gives an indication of the great strength of the sealant.

Glue and pin a suitable moulding around the edges of the baseboard as shown, and touch up the woodwork if necessary with wood dye before applying at least two coats of polyurethane lacquer (*Figure 106*).

The case will remain securely on the baseboard by its own weight, but, as said earlier, some form of fixing should be incorporated. One method of providing this is to cut away part of the shortened leg of the timber angle at the base of the frame near two diagonally opposite corners to make enough space to receive a square nut, which can be attached by using the silicone sealant or epoxy resin. Carefully mark off the location of these fixings on the baseboard rebate, and drill slightly oversized holes to take the corresponding slot-headed bolts. Invert the baseboard and countersink the holes sufficiently to allow the bolt-heads to lie below the surface. The method of fixing the case to the baseboard once the model has been mounted is to allow one end of the baseboard to project over the edge of a table while the bolt is inserted and lightly tightened.

There are a number of methods of mounting the model on the baseboard, and the one chosen must, of course, have been taken into consideration when calculating the height of the case. Brass dolphins, ornamental figures or turned brass pillars can be found at good model shops. These can be secured to the baseboard by means of decorative screws which have projecting pegs for insertion into corresponding holes in the keel of the model. Alternatively, a hardwood cradle can be made with padded supports, the dimensions for which are obtained by referring to the body plan. The extent of decorative moulding on the cradle is purely a matter of choice, but it should not detract from the model. The model of *Sirius* sits on a series of plain wooden blocks representing the baulks of timber which are used in a dry dock (*see Figure 1*). Once the mountings have been fixed in position, the whole baseboard should be given two or three coats of polyurethane lacquer, and in this instance a gloss finish may be considered,

as it will bring out the best in the wood you have used.

Nameplate

This item will be the final addition to the display before closing up the case. You may wish to indicate just the name and date of the vessel, and it is possible that your model shop will have a stock of ready-made brass nameplates to meet your need. If not, you might try your hand at engraving, or have a nameplate specially made. If, however, you would like the satisfaction of producing your own professional-looking nameplate, you should consider the method set out below.

A piece of brass sheet perhaps 0.25mm thick and about 100mm × 50mm (4in × 2in) is bonded to a slightly larger piece of obeche or lime sheet, 2 or 3mm thick, using epoxy resin glue. The surface of the brass is covered with masking tape on which is drawn the outline of the desired shape, and this is then carefully fretsawed out using a fretsaw blade designed for cutting metal. This will leave smooth clean edges which may then be painted matt black. The masking tape is then stripped off and the brass polished with Brasso, after which any grease is cleaned off with methylated spirits. The lettering in the form of Letraset or other instant lettering may now be applied, but, in order to achieve proper adherence of the letters, a fine coat of matt lacquer must first be sprayed over the surface from an aerosol can. Allow the lacquer to dry completely, apply the lettering, and spray several more protective coats of lacquer over the surface, noting the manufacturers' recommendations regarding intervals between coats. The whole plate may then be fixed with pva adhesive to a suitable hardwood block, which is then gloss lacquered to an attractive finish. The completed nameplate assembly is then secured to the baseboard by screws or glue (*Figure 107*).

You may wish to include some notes on the history of the vessel or comments on the construction of the model. These should be neatly typed out, using, if possible, an

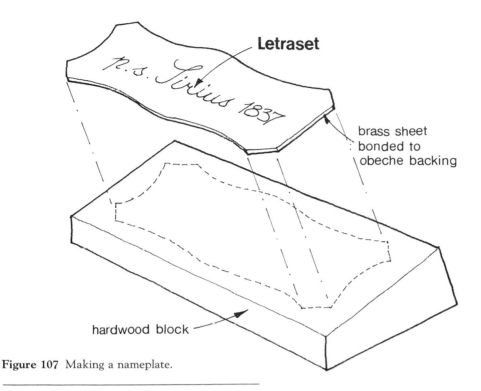

Letraset

brass sheet
bonded to
obeche backing

hardwood block

Figure 107 Making a nameplate.

italicised or other special typeface, and reduced on a photocopier to about half size. The paper can then be glued to a hardwood block and located in the display case in such a way as not to obstruct the view of the model.

Modelling sea

A scenic or waterline model should be set in a representation of the sea. Each modeller tends to have a favoured method of modelling water, and, judging by the difficulty in obtaining information on the subject, the secrets are closely-guarded. Two methods will be described here, one for calm water and one for rough. In either case you will have constructed your model with the hull truncated just below the waterline.

Rough water
In rough weather, or when under way, your ship will almost certainly be heeling over to a certain extent. You should limit the amount of heel to a few degrees on all but the smallest models, or you may have to increase the size of the display case considerably. Cut two wooden wedges no longer than the width of the hull, set them in position on the baseboard, and try your model on them. When you are satisfied with the attitude of the ship, glue the wedges in position on the baseboard. After allowing the glue to set, drill a hole down through each wedge and right through the baseboard, with a countersinking underneath. Set the model in position and push a sharp instrument, such as a gimlet, up through each hole to mark the position of the fixing holes on the base of the model. Drill these fixing holes for the screw size you intend to use.

Your baseboard will need to have raised edges to contain the 'sea'. Select a piece of obeche $\frac{1}{4}$in (6mm) thick, wide enough to mask the edges of the baseboard and to extend about $\frac{1}{2}$in (12mm) above it. Countersink screw and glue four pieces of this material to the baseboard, and glue and mitre the corners. Now drill a random pattern of small holes over the whole baseboard except for the area covered by the model. The holes should be 2½– 3in apart (65–75mm). Drive a ½in (12mm) countersunk steel screw into each hole, leaving about ¼in (6mm) projecting above the baseboard. The purpose of these screws is to prevent the 'sea' from coming loose and curling up. Now give the whole sea container a coat of polyurethane varnish to prevent moisture from getting into the baseboard and frame (*Figure 108*).

You will need a quantity of papier mâché. Tear up several large sheets of newspaper to the smallest size commensurate with your patience, and mix them with water in a bucket. The mixture should have the consistency of thick porridge, and should be free from lumps. Add two tablespoons of wallpaper adhesive to the mixture, and set it aside for at least 24 hours. When you are satisfied that you have a really smooth papier mâché, apply it in handfuls to the baseboard and mould it into the shapes of waves as desired. Work it around the hull carefully to obtain the formation which a ship in motion would produce – for this you will need to study pictures or models of the subject. Avoid excessive thickness, which may cause the material to crack as it dries. When you have achieved a good result, remove the fixing screws and, without disturbing the sea, carefully lift the model free. Unnecessary contact between the ship and the wet papier mâché is to be avoided.

Set the baseboard in a warm, dry place and leave it undisturbed for at least a week. When it is completely dry and hard, you may exercise your artistic talents in painting the grey mass to look like swirling, choppy water. Use a flat, oil-based paint in soft sea-shades, allowing the colours to run together and mingle to create the right appearance. A few brushlines of white along the crests of some of the waves, blended back into the surrounding water look effective. If your first attempt is not altogether successful, there is no need to despair, as once the paint has dried you may try again. However, you must avoid fiddling too long with a reasonable attempt, as a point is reached when your efforts will detract from the result, rather than improve it. When the sea-scape eventually meets the approval of your critical eye, apply two or three generous coats of clear gloss or satin polyurethane varnish to give the effect of depth. Once the varnish is dry, the model can be set in position for the last time, and the fixing screws tightened.

Calm water
If your ship is moored or becalmed, it is likely that she would sit on an even keel. The hull can thus be fixed flat, using two screws which are countersunk into the underside of the baseboard. Mark the outline of the base of the model in pencil onto the baseboard, then remove the model.

Mix a small quantity of white filler in accordance with the manufacturer's instructions. A suitable material is Tetrion All-purpose Filler, made by Tetrosyl Limited, Bury, Lancashire, England. Apply the filler to the baseboard with an old kitchen-knife, working in small areas, as the material dries very quickly. Smooth it out, lifting the knife at the end of each stroke to give the effect of ripples. Small disturbances can be introduced by wiping the wet filler with a finger. Take care not to go beyond the pencil outline of the hull, or the model will not sit squarely on the baseboard. When the filler has set hard, paint in your sea-scape, using flat oil-based paint. Bear in mind that calm water has fewer colour variations than rough. Finally, apply varnish as described for rough water, and fix the model in position.

Location

Avoid locating the display in areas subject to strong sunlight or near radiators or other heat sources, for these contribute to deterioration. If space is available, an all-round view of the model is ideal, illustrating, if nothing else, that

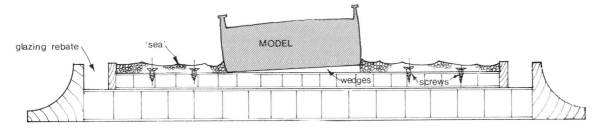

Figure 108 Section through a waterline model on its baseboard surrounded by a papier mâché sea. The screws are inserted to prevent the sea from curling or becoming loose.

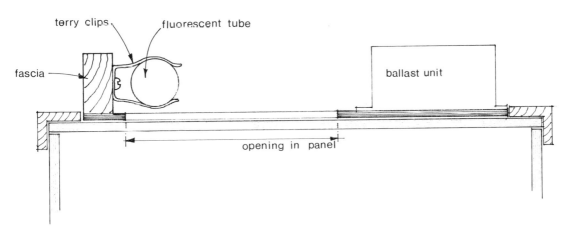

Figure 109 Section through a removable fluorescent lighting panel fitted in the top of the glass case.

you have lavished as much care on the starboard side as on the port. Some form of room divider with shelves would provide a suitable location, and indeed, the glazing may simply be applied to the two sides of such an open fitting rather than constructing a separate display case. More frequently, however, it is necessary to set the display case against a wall, permitting only a one-sided view of the model. You may be able to obtain from your hardware shop a pair of wall brackets which are fixed by drilling a $\frac{3}{8}$ in (10mm) hole into the wall to receive the steel prong welded to the back of each bracket. These brackets have the advan-

tage of being virtually invisible below the baseboard, and are therefore not as unsightly as the more common gallows-type bracket. They are stated to be capable of carrying 120lbs (55kg) each, which should be more than adequate.

Lighting

Quite often the natural and artificial lighting arrangements in a room are sufficient for the display of the model. However, the effect of a well-lit model in a room with subdued lighting is dramatic, and you may well feel inclined to go to a little trouble and expense in order to provide a form of lighting which will enhance the appearance of your handiwork.

Assuming that the display has been located with the top of the case a little above eye level, a 4mm ($\frac{3}{16}$in) plywood or hardboard panel is cut to fit inside the top frame of the case. An opening is made in this panel leaving about 75mm (3in) at the back and at each side, and 10mm ($\frac{3}{8}$in) along the front. Along this front edge is fixed a 20mm ($\frac{3}{4}$in) × 10mm ($\frac{3}{8}$in) fascia of obeche or other timber which can be stained and lacquered to match the framing of the case.

A standard miniature fluorescent tube, 15mm ($\frac{5}{8}$in) in diameter and 530mm (21in) long, is fixed by means of two terry clips to the back of the fascia, and the ballast equipment glued with epoxy resin to the back of the panel (*Figure 109*). Epoxy is also used to spot-fix the cables neatly out of sight. It may be necessary to use small cable clips on the back of one of the case frames if the power cable has to be led down below the baseboard, and, if so, it is recommended that the holes for the clip pins be drilled rather than hammering the clips in.

This arrangement gives a good quality strong light downwards onto the model while screening the light source from the observer. It is satisfactory where the display case has been located against a wall; but if all-round viewing is possible, the method can be adapted by constructing an enclosed ventilated housing for the fluorescent tube and ballast. The size of the opening in the top panel will have to be adjusted to give optimum results.

Glossary

Abeam On a line at right angles to the ship's length

Aft Towards the stern of the vessel

Amidships The middle of the ship

Backstays Stays leading from the tops of the upper masts to fixing points aft of the mast on the sides of the vessel

Beam The width of a vessel

Bend To tie by means of rope or line

Block A pulley in a frame, with an eye for the attachment of a line

Boom A spar to which the foot of a fore-and-aft sail is bent

Bow The forend of a ship

Bowsprit A spar extending forward from the stem of a ship

Braces Ropes used to adjust yards to the required sailing angle

Bulkheads Vertical partitions dividing the hull into compartments

Bulwarks The frames and planking which extend above the main deck

Cannon Ships' guns

Capstan A vertical winch for handling heavy cables and ropes

Careen To pull a vessel over onto its side by means of cables attached to the superstructure in order to carry out maintenance on the bottom

Catheads Timbers projecting on either side of the bow used to support the anchors before they are secured

Caulk To force tarred rope fibres into the seams of planking in order to make it watertight

Chain plates Iron plates bolted to the ship's sides below the chain wales; the lower deadeyes are attached to the top of the chain plates

Companionway Steep staircase leading below decks

Cutwater Forward edge of the stem of a ship

Davits Iron or timber members which support ships' boats

Deadeyes Circular wooden blocks with a grooved circumference, thrice drilled through the face

Doubling Additional timbers located between frames to give extra strength

Fighting top On early vessels, the platform built at the lower masthead to accommodate archers or sharpshooters

Floors Transverse beams between the keel and keelson

Foot ropes Rope loops suspended beneath yards on which crew could stand or move when working on the sails

Footrope The rope sewn to the lower edge of a sail

Fore-and-aft sails Sails set in the direction of the length of the ship

Forecastle A raised deck forward of the foremast

Foremast The mast nearest the bow of a ship with two or more masts

Forward In the direction of the bow of a ship

Frames The ribs of a ship's hull

Furl To roll up and bind a sail to a yard

Gaff Spar to which the head of a fore-and-aft sail is bent

Glass A period of 30 minutes, or one-eighth of a four-hour watch

Halliard Hoisting rope for a yard or sail

Hatch An opening in the deck of a ship

Hawse-hole Opening in the bow through which the anchor cable passes

Jib Fore-and-aft sail set on a stay forward of the foremast

Keel The lowest longitudinal member of the hull, from which the frames rise

Keelson Longitudinal member parallel to and above the keel, separated from the keel by the floor timbers

Lanyard Rope or line threaded through deadeyes, and used to apply tension to the shrouds

Lateen sail A triangular sail on a centrally-suspended yard sloped at 45° to the mast

Lee The side away from the direction of the wind

Mainmast The middle mast on a three-masted vessel, or the aftermast on a two-master

Messenger A light, endless line usually taken round a capstan and used for hauling a heavier rope or hawse

Midships *see* Amidships

Mizzen The aftermast of a three-masted vessel, or the third mast on a vessel of more than three masts

Nippers Short lines used to fasten a heavy rope or hawse to a messenger

Poop Short aftermost deck over the quarterdeck

Port 1) The left side of a ship facing forward
2) An opening in the side of a ship

Preventer An additional or safety fastening

Quarter Either side of a ship near the stern

Quarterdeck The part of the upper deck between the stern and aftermast

Rate Early means of denoting the class and gunpower of a ship

Reef To reduce the area of sail by partially tying it up to the yard

Running free Sailing with the wind astern or on either quarter

Running rigging Rigging used to operate the yards and sails

Scarf A joint formed by notching two pieces of timber so that they overlap without an increase in thickness

Sheet A rope from the lower corner of a square sail, staysail or jib, or boom, used to control the set of the sail

Shrouds Ropes running from the masthead to deadeyes at the ship's sides

Seize Fasten or attach by binding with cord

Spar General term for masts, yards etc.

Square sail Four-cornered sail extended on a yard slung centrally on the mast

Standing rigging The fixed rigging of a ship which secures the masts

Starboard The right side of a ship facing forward

Stays Forward-running ropes which support the masts

Staysail A sail set on a stay

Stem The foremost vertical timber of a ship's hull

Stern The aftermost part of a ship

Sternpost The aftermost vertical timber of a ship's hull

Tack The lower forward corner of a fore-and-aft sail

Tiller A lever which moves in a horizontal plane, used to turn the rudder from side to side

Topgallant mast The mast above the topmast

Topmast The mast above the lower mast

Top The assembly at the lower masthead

Tumblehome The inward rake of the sides of a ship

Turnbuckle Device consisting of two threaded rods set in line in an iron fitting, used for applying tension to a cable

Wales Broad, thick timbers running fore-and-aft along a ship's side

Windlass Horizontal winch for handling heavy cables and ropes

Windward The side towards the wind

Yards Spars on which square sails are set

Maritime museums in the USA

The Mariners Museum, Newport News, Virginia

This important museum houses a large collection of naval material from all over the world, including paintings, plans and rigged models. An extensive library covers maritime documents, ships' plans and photographs.

United States National Museum (Smithsonian Institute), Washington, D.C.

Smaller craft such as fishing schooners and pilot boats are a feature of this museum, but there are also a few models of clippers. There is a rich collection of plans of American merchant sailing ships, catalogued in great detail in *The National Waterfront Collection*.

Peabody Museum, Salem, Mass.

The exhibits at this museum are principally concerned with sailing vessels built in Salem and New England. A large collection of historical photographs and ships' plans are on display, together with paintings by the famous French marine artist Roux.

San Francisco Maritime Museum, San Francisco, Calif.

The museum deals with the tradition and history of modern seafaring, with emphasis on the Pacific. There is a large collection of models of schooners and square-rigged vessels, together with a display of paintings and ships' plans. There is also a nautical library with a photographic display. The restored iron-hulled *Balclutha* lies fully rigged in San Francisco harbour, close by to the museum.

Marine Historical Association Inc., Mystic, Conn.

Here is a fine collection of models of rigged sailing ships and steamships, as well as prints, paintings and plans, particularly relating to those built in Connecticut. There is also a major collection of paintings by the French marine artist Roux.

Appendix

On the following pages is a set of drawings which is intended to show the extent of information required for the basic construction of a ½in scale model ship. The paddle steamer *Sirius* has been chosen, as there are many references to this vessel in the foregoing text. In addition to this information, you will need to carry out your own research into colours and finishes. In the case of this model, some 20 colour photographs of the ½in scale model in the Science Museum were a useful source of information, and cross-checks were made against paintings and line drawings of the ship.

It would be possible to construct a model of the *Sirius* from these drawings, although there is no doubt that the best way of achieving accuracy is to obtain a set of drawings to the correct scale from one of the sources given. The body plan and details of deck fittings are reproduced to the correct scale, and may be scaled or traced off as required. The spar drawings, which are smaller than scale size, are fully dimensioned, and should present no difficulties. The elevation and plan of the deck, while greatly reduced, are nevertheless provided with a scale from which the location of the bulkheads and deck fittings may be determined.

If you follow the method described for bulkhead construction and the subsequent sections on fixtures, fittings and rigging, you should experience no great difficulty in finding the information you need to complete your model.

The paddle steamer *Sirius* was the first vessel to cross the Atlantic under continuous steam power. She was built by Robert Menzies and Son of Leith for service between London and Cork, and was operated by the St George Steam Packet Company. In April 1838 she was chartered by the British and American Steamship Navigation Company, whose own ship, the p.s. *British Queen*, was not ready in time; and she was despatched from London to New York. Competition was great, and the *Sirius* arrived in New York harbour only a few hours before Brunel's p.s. *Great Western*, whose departure had been delayed by unfavourable weather.

The vessel was propelled by two 320hp side-lever engines, with two 60in diameter cylinders of 6ft stroke. She was the first steamer to be fitted with surface condensers, allowing the boilers to be fed with fresh water. The rectangular flue boilers consumed 24 tons of coal per day, and top speed under ideal conditions was 9 knots.

Gross register:	703 tons
Burden:	412 tons
Draft:	15ft

Overall length:	208ft 0in
Breadth of hull:	25ft 7in
Over paddle boxes:	47ft 3in

110

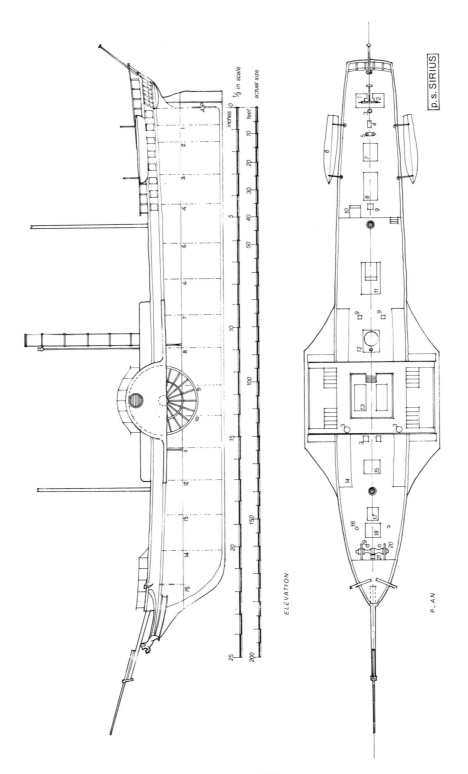

ELEVATION

PLAN

p.s. SIRIUS

Figure 110 Plan and elevation of p.s. *Sirius*

111

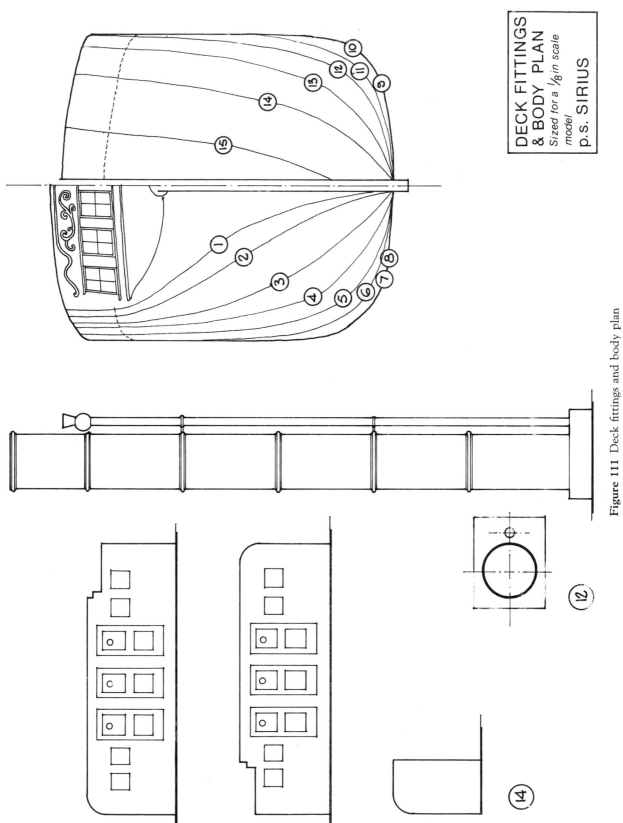

DECK FITTINGS
& BODY PLAN
*Sized for a ⅛ in scale
model*
p.s. SIRIUS

Figure 111 Deck fittings and body plan

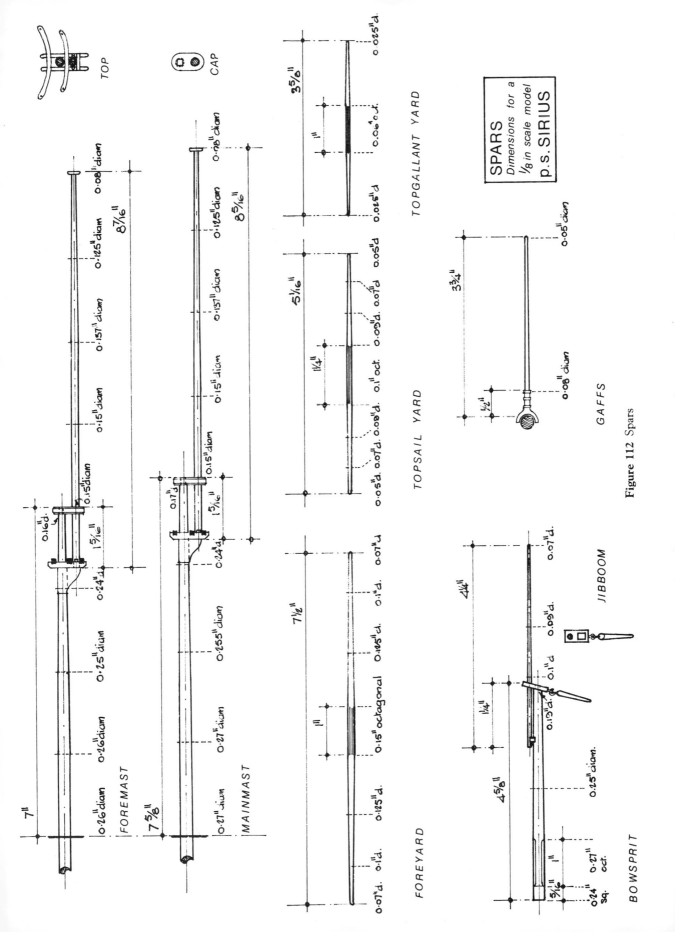

TOP

CAP

SPARS
Dimensions for a
⅛ in scale model
p.s. SIRIUS

FOREMAST

MAINMAST

TOPGALLANT YARD

TOPSAIL YARD

GAFFS

FOREYARD

JIBBOOM

BOWSPRIT

Figure 112 Spars

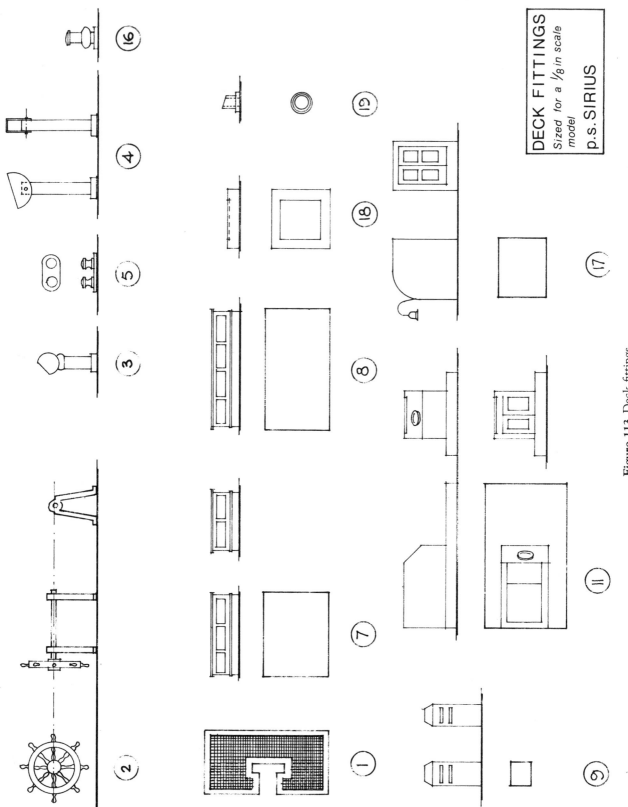

Figure 113 Deck fittings

DECK FITTINGS
Sized for a 1/8 in scale model
p.s. SIRIUS

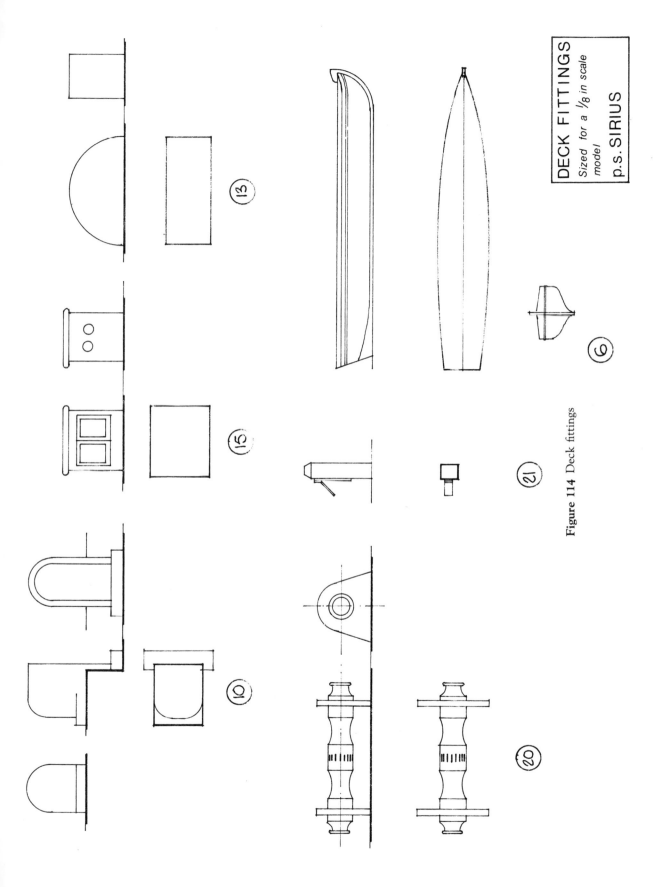

DECK FITTINGS
Sized for a $\frac{1}{8}$ in scale model
p.s. SIRIUS

Figure 114 Deck fittings

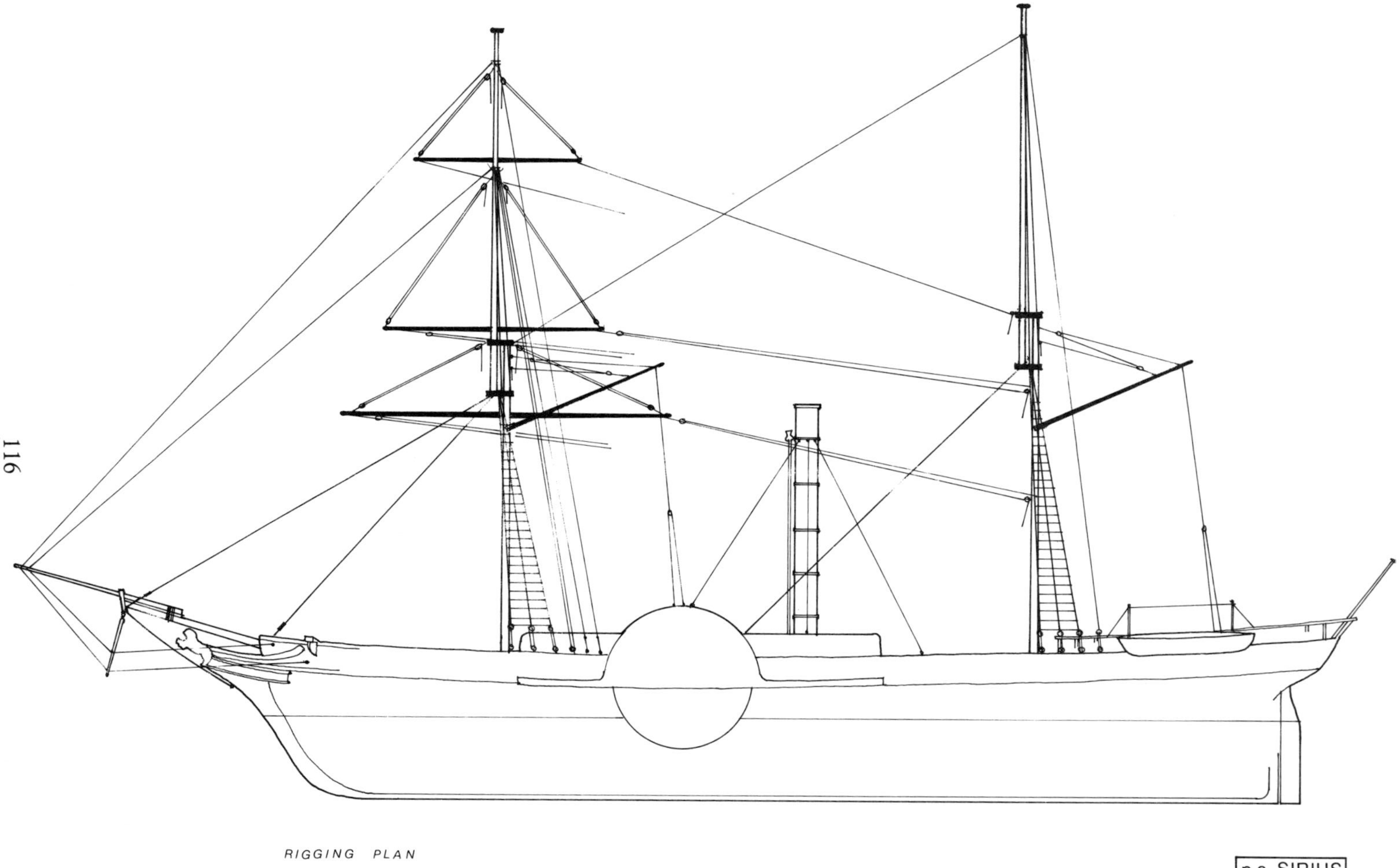

RIGGING PLAN

p.s. SIRIUS

Figure 115 Rigging plan

116

Index

Numbers in italics refer to pages on which illustrations appear